Visual Thinking

Tools for Mapping Your Ideas

Nancy Margulies and Christine Valenza

Crown House Publishing Company LLC
www.CHPUS.com

Visual Thinking
Tools for Mapping Your Ideas

Grades 4–12 and adult

© 2005 by Nancy Margulies and Christine Valenza Reprinted 2006
Printed in the United States of America

ISBN: 1-904424-56-2 13 digit ISBN: 978-1904424567

Published by:
Crown House Publishing Company LLC
4 Berkeley Street
Norwalk, CT 06850
www.CHPUS.com
Tel: 866-272-8497
Fax: 203-852-9619
E-mail: info@CHPUS.com

Editing: Melanie Mallon
Design, typesetting, and cover: Dan Miedaner

Library of Congress Control Number: 2004111450

In a climate where more and more students are having learning problems, the Visual Thinking *method is one of the most valuable tools I am aware of. I have seen it in operation and cannot recommend it highly enough.*

—Mona Brookes
founder of Monart Drawing Schools, author of *Drawing with Children*

Visual Thinking *is a wonderful, inviting workbook that gives you the basic tools for "speaking" visual language, a language I have predicted will be a new international auxiliary language. With this book, nobody has an excuse like "but I can't draw." With* Visual Thinking *anybody can begin to put thoughts in graphic form. And teachers, parents, and kids will delight in the ease and fun of doing it. The authors have provided easy-to-follow tips for drawing, over 500 simple-to-draw icons and visual symbols, and more than a dozen templates for putting together ideas to create and convey larger patterns of thoughts.*

—Robert E. Horn
author of *Visual Language: Global Communication for the 21st Century*

A helpful hands-on tool for classroom teachers and group facilitators. Those of us who are artistically challenged will particularly love using this book! Immediately usable.

—Patt Sheldon
veteran teacher, former Beginning-Teacher Support and
Assessment Advisor, currently teaching sixth grade

This book reawakens the powerful part of us that is the image maker, a resource that often lies dormant and unused. Visual Thinking *is an excellent tool for teachers, tutors, and parents, who are working with students that are primarily visual learners in school systems that are not always designed for them. This is also a practical guide for anyone working with students with learning differences and looking for new ways to bring information.*

—Karen Nani Apana, Ph.D.
San Francisco Waldorf High School Faculty and High School Mentor

Refreshingly simple, Visual Thinking *provides a potent and easily implemented visual lesson plan in problem solving and critical thinking. With practical applications for any organization, it is especially useful for children as they navigate in a complex world. The real power in* Visual Thinking *lies in the possibilities for deeper thinking, understanding, and more effective communication.*

—Mary Corrigan
graphic facilitator

Contents

FOR INSPIRATION

• Geoff Ball
• Susan Kelly
• Jennifer Hammond-Landau
• David Sibbet
• Tom Benthin
• Jan Adkins

The International Forum of Visual Practitioners

For INSPIRING and GUIDING us.

• RONNIE DURIE

Thank you!

• MELANIE MALLON
Our Editor

FAMILY, FRIENDS and COLLEAGUES

• MICHELLE BOOS-STONE
• NUSA MAAL
• ALBERT
• HELEN SPECTOR
• JOAN
Dee Dickinson
• GARY

NEW HORIZONS for LEARNING

newhorizons.org

6

Foreword

In my office one afternoon in the winter of 1988, I received a telephone call from someone who identified herself as Nancy Margulies. She told me she was calling from St. Louis and would like to make an appointment to see me in Seattle about some new skills she had developed. She had heard about New Horizons for Learning and thought we might find them useful. I had come to expect the unexpected in my work with New Horizons for Learning and said I would be happy to meet with her. She flew in the next day, enthusiastically explained her skills, and asked if she could accompany me to demonstrate them as I did some workshops for teachers. As she spent the week demonstrating her Mindscaping techniques, we all saw possibilities for powerful new ways of enhancing teaching and learning.

At that time, we were in the process of planning a conference called "Creating the Future of Education" and invited Nancy to Mindscape each of the presentations. That summer at George Mason University, Nancy worked her magic, drawing rapidly with colorful markers on a large pad of paper that sat on an easel beside the podium. Each day we posted in the auditorium a visual record of each presentation, and at the end of the conference, the participants left with a little booklet of the Mindscapes that recorded highlights of what they had experienced.

That was the beginning of Nancy Margulies's remarkable career, which has taken her throughout the world from educational conferences to corporate board rooms to meetings of the U.S. President's cabinet, and from India at a special meeting with the Dalai Lama to New Zealand, working with aborigines, to working with the World Cafe. In all cases, these visual representations of sometimes abstract ideas have made them more easily understood and memorable.

Coauthor Christine Valenza and Nancy began working together ten years ago, combining their complementary skills. Christine has applied her abilities in mapping and visual thinking nationally and internationally with corporate and nonprofit organizations, focusing on facilitating learning, meaning making, and decision making. She also trains youth to work with her in international multicultural projects.

This unique book is invaluable in helping both students and educators to learn skills that are appropriate for communicating in any culture in today's increasingly visual world. Mindscaping also facilitates learning by incorporating all learning styles—auditory as people listen more keenly, and visual, kinesthetic, and symbolic as they create patterns and make connections. As a result, important new careers are being launched. Mindscaping is a new kind of literacy that we would all do well to master, and this practical handbook is all we need to get started as well as to become more proficient in using techniques that are critically important for our times.

—Dee Dickinson, Chief Learning Officer,
New Horizons for Learning, www.newhorizons.org

Introduction

This book is a response to requests from teachers and parents around the globe for more ways to use visual mapping to enhance thinking skills and for a greater resource for finding and creating symbols. Many teachers have discovered that mapping ideas helps them communicate with students by creating engaging, memorable experiences. Students find the process of visually recording ideas, whether for taking notes or creating presentations, to be more fun than traditional written recording, such as linear note taking. By mapping the ideas, students can record new ideas where they fit in terms of content. This process enables students to organize their notes by category and relationship while mapping. See, for example, the maps that capture science lessons, on pages 21–23, and the map about ancient Egypt, on page 25. Not only is the process more memorable and fun, the results are excellent review tools. It's far easier for students to remember a symbol than a string of words.

Although the benefits of visual mapping have long been established, one of the most important aspects of making ideas visible is often overlooked. Making ideas visible, using both words and images, means that we are making our very process of thinking visible. Often we go about thinking and attempting to solve problems without a conscious awareness of our own process. This is much like trying to maneuver your way through a crowded room in total darkness. You stumble blindly along, hoping that your memory of the room is accurate. Much of what goes on in our minds that is usually unavailable to us—that is, in fact, invisible—becomes knowable when it leaves the far reaches of our brains and shows up on paper. Once our ideas exist outside our brains, we can explore them in greater depth. This capacity to work with ideas made visible is an important aspect of visual intelligence (McGuinness 2003).

Visually mapping ideas is a process that allows you to see the parts and the whole and notice the relationship between them. Often our minds move from detail to detail without the ability to step back and see the entire system. Once ideas are poured onto paper and made visible, the big picture comes into focus.

Whether you are new to visual mapping or an experienced Mindscaper, this book will bring you a wealth of symbols and templates to use for mapping, creating worksheets, making the chalkboard or whiteboard more

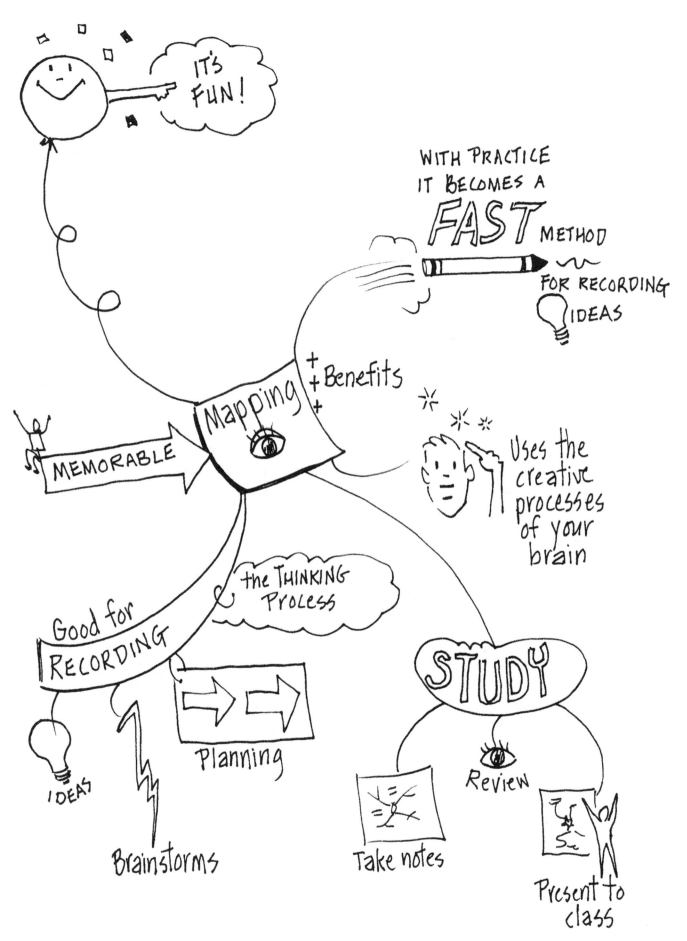

appealing and meaningful, and teaching your students how to create symbols to express their own ideas. (Note: Except when we discuss Mindscapes specifically, we generally refer to Mindscaping, Mind Mapping, visual organizers, graphic organizers, clustering, and other note-taking systems for visually representing ideas as "maps" and "mapping." We use the term "symbols" to represent any image that conveys an idea.)

Visual Language

Man has functioned as a seer and embraced vastness for millennia. But only recently, through television and the modern media, have we been able to shift from the clumsiness of speech as a means of expression and therefore of communication, to the powers of infinite visual expression, thus enabling us to share with everybody the immense dynamic wholes in no time.

—Caleb Gattegno, *Towards a Visual Culture*

The integration of images and words creates powerful visual languages. Have you ever noticed that as you think, images come to mind? Students' capacity to think through complex problems is enhanced when they can see the process on paper. Using the Mindscapes provided in this book, students will be better able to organize their thoughts. The ideas a child may have about how to accomplish a certain goal, for example, may be floating in his or her head outside the realm of awareness. Once they are on paper in a fashion that shows their relationship to one another, ideas become clearer and easier to manipulate. Mental energy is freed to examine the combination of thoughts and to plan next steps.

Throughout history human beings have used images—cave paintings, icons, pictographs—to express their thoughts. Pictographs (pictures representing ideas, as in primitive writing) and hieroglyphics are among the oldest forms of visual language. The Sumerians in 4000 BCE used over 2,000 pictographs in their writing. In our modern world, the addition of visual images to our work can clarify context and meaning between us and our students. Symbols that express specific meaning have been used for centuries in disciplines such as science, mathematics, music, and dance. As we develop international symbols and recognize the value of visual intelligence, more symbols appear daily. As people who speak different languages come together in a global culture, it is natural that we invent a new language that can convey complex ideas using images as well as text.

The Evolution of Images

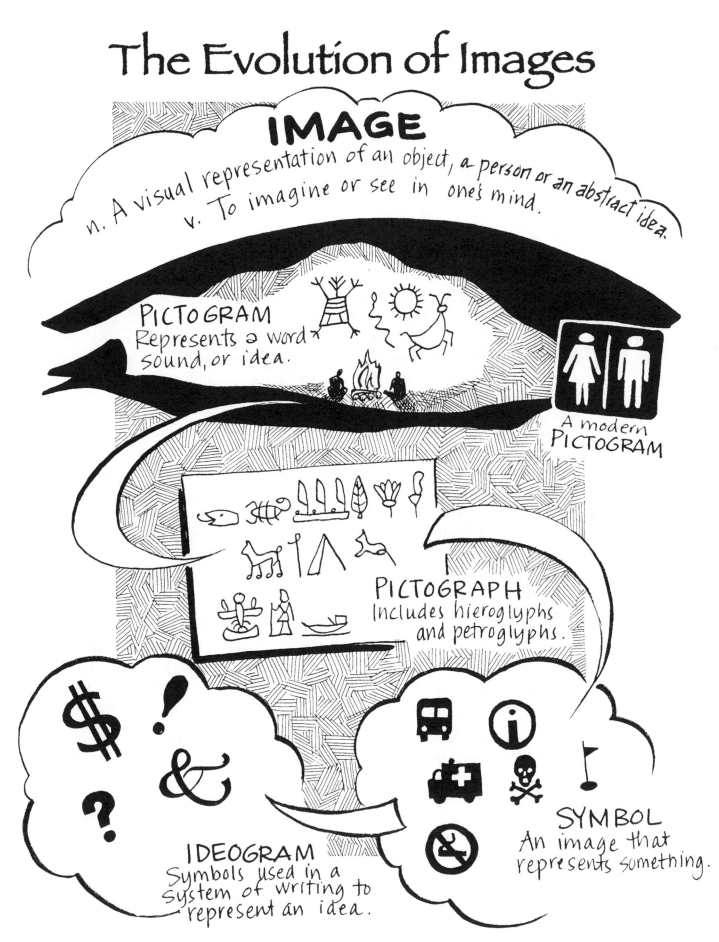

IMAGE

n. A visual representation of an object, a person or an abstract idea.
v. To imagine or see in one's mind.

PICTOGRAM
Represents a word, sound, or idea.

A modern PICTOGRAM

PICTOGRAPH
Includes hieroglyphs and petroglyphs.

IDEOGRAM
Symbols used in a system of writing to represent an idea.

SYMBOL
An image that represents something.

Visuals can condense extensive amounts of information and are often comprehended regardless of age or culture. When you are able to bring simple images into the classroom you enrich the learning environment.

About This Book

The use of visual tools creates a shift in classroom dynamics from passive to interactive learning for all to see.

—David Hyerle, *Visual Tools for Constructing Knowledge*

Chapter 1 introduces the many uses and approaches to basic Mindscaping, the simplest and most free-form visual recording method. In addition to an introduction of how mapping will benefit you and your students, the chapter details the steps for creating a Mindscape, with examples of Mindscaped student reports and an example outline to illustrate the practical and effective use of Mindscapes in the classroom.

Chapter 2 walks you and your students through basic drawing techniques that anyone can use to create symbols, even if you think you can't draw. Use this chapter to build your own confidence and photocopy the pages to use as handouts for your students. For many adults and older students, the idea of drawing stands like a giant boulder in our paths marked "No, you can't." Chapter 2 will enable you to sidestep the boulder and continue blazing a new trail. You will be able to prepare worksheets, make posters, and convey ideas in a manner that appeals to your students, especially those students for whom reading is challenging.

In chapter 3, you will find a "symbolary," which provides you with hundreds of simple images you and your students can draw to convey a variety of ideas. Next to each symbol are words that it could represent, although this list is by no means exhaustive. You are encouraged to use these symbols *with* written words to reinforce your point and lessen the chance of confusion.

Hand-drawn symbols can be applied to a range of subjects and do not need to be taught as a separate unit. However, for those students interested in drawing, you can hand out the symbol-drawing pages to give them an opportunity to copy the images and create symbols of their own. When the book *Mapping Inner Space* was published, many teachers wrote to say that with the introduction of simple maps, their most challenging students were transformed into the most engaged. Other students, who are less confident, may wish to begin with the step-by-step symbol drawing on pages 40 and 41.

We are living in a culture that is communicating with more icons and symbols than ever before. Encourage your students to notice the symbols in their world. You may want to begin a collection of symbols copied from magazines or seen on the computer screen. Students may be more symbol-savvy than you think. They encounter symbols when using e-mail, using electronic equipment of all sorts, and reading common signs, such as those indicating disabled parking, ladies' and men's rooms, no smoking, and a host of other everyday symbols. Take a look at the common symbols we see around us daily, shown on page 153. We will also introduce you to the world of clip art graphics that are relevant to lesson planning and encourage you to explore those resources.

Chapter 4 provides you with a number of ways to use symbols with templates to enrich your students' thinking skills. We have designed the templates so that students can fill them in and, in doing so, move through stages of thinking and problem solving. With younger children, you can show the map and ask the questions, filling in the map for them, using words and pictures. Mapping in this way can be applied across the curriculum. In both cases (whether students use the templates or you work through them as a class), the steps in the thinking process become more clear, and students can slow down the thinking process in order to be more thorough and skillful. Armed with stronger thinking skills and visual recording methods, your students will find note taking, studying, review, and all learning tasks to be easier, more fun, and more memorable, and they will soon see a difference in their ability to retain and understand what they learn and to apply their enhanced abilities on tests and other assessments.

The resources section will lead you to books, organizations, and other sources for delving deeper into the teaching of thinking skills, the use of visual language, and mapping for classroom use.

Chapter 1

Making Mindscapes

Whether conscious of it or not, we all devote most of our mental energy to visually interpreting our surroundings.

—Oliver Caviglioli and Ian Harris, *Thinking Skills and Eye Q*

Mindscapes are visual representations of ideas using images and words. Some Mindscapes are visual metaphors, or templates, such as the image of a person climbing a mountain to represent achieving a goal. Other Mindscapes are more free form—in fact, any configuration is acceptable. The process is similar to Mind Mapping, but with fewer restrictions. Mind Mapping, developed by British author Tony Buzan, always begins in the center of the page, with lines branching out from there. One word is allowed per line. The result looks somewhat like a web of diagrammed sentences with symbols added.

Because they can easily be shared, maps lend themselves well to group work and presentations to the class, in addition to being useful for individual note taking, study, and review. A map enables the viewer to see the whole picture as well as the individual aspects and encourages students to think not only in terms of the information they wish to impart but also in terms of the relationship among ideas.

The following information is presented here (and on page 16) in written form and on the opposite page in Mindscape form. As you can see, the information presented visually engages the reader in a dynamic and compelling manner.

"The process of developing and using a graphic organizer has been shown to enhance students' critical thinking and higher order thinking skills" (IARE 2003, 9). Twenty-nine research studies show that the use of graphic organizers (such as Mindscapes, Mind Maps, and other visual recordings) helps students

- brainstorm ideas
- develop, organize, and communicate ideas
- see connections, patterns, and relationships
- assess and share prior knowledge
- develop vocabulary

29 RESEARCH

Research studies show that using graphic organizers (like Mindscapes & templates) helps students:

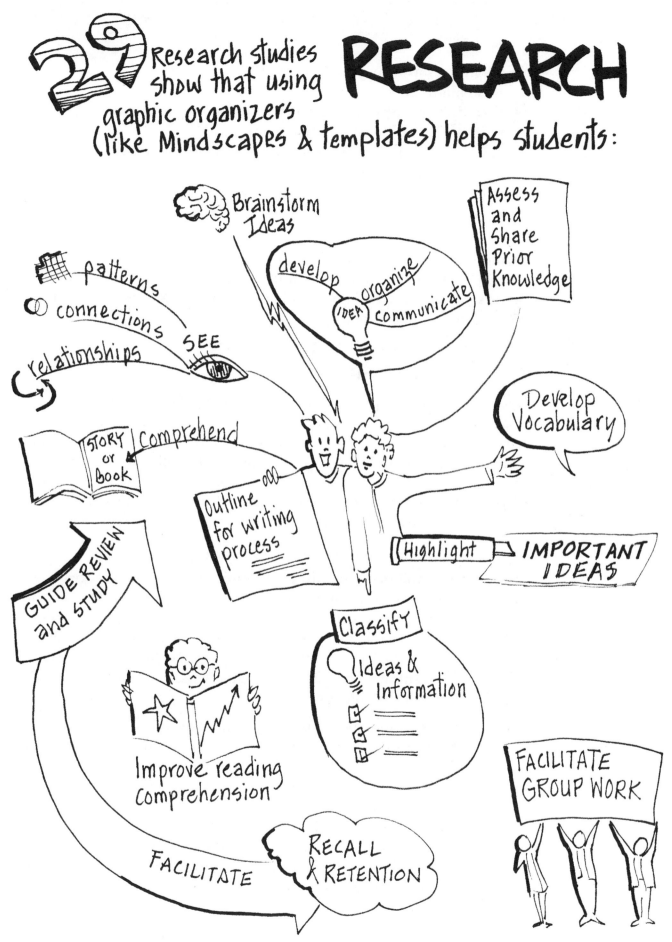

- Brainstorm Ideas
- develop — organize — communicate IDEA
- Assess and Share Prior Knowledge
- see patterns, connections, relationships
- Develop Vocabulary
- Comprehend Story or Book
- Outline for writing process
- Highlight IMPORTANT IDEAS
- GUIDE REVIEW and STUDY
- Improve reading comprehension
- Classify Ideas & Information
- FACILITATE GROUP WORK
- FACILITATE Recall & Retention

- outline for writing process activities
- highlight important ideas
- classify or categorize concepts, ideas, and information
- comprehend the events in a story or book
- improve social interactions and facilitate group work
- guide review and study
- improve reading comprehension skills and strategies
- facilitate recall and retention
  (IARE 2003)

In addition, Mindscapes are useful for problem solving, event planning, setting (and achieving) goals, and preparing and giving oral or written reports. In fact, as you will see later in this chapter, a Mindscape can be an effective report in and of itself.

Mindscaping Steps

The soul never thinks without a mental image.

—Aristotle

There are as many approaches to Mindscaping as there are uses. One approach is to fill in an existing template (such as one of the many templates in chapter 4). Another approach is to begin with a large blank sheet of paper. We find that 11" x 17" paper works well, but you might also try using flipchart paper or a roll of butcher paper, or just draw your Mindscape on the board. A set of markers in at least four different colors is ideal when working on paper; use colored chalk if working on a chalkboard.

The steps for Mindscaping are straightforward:

1. Draw a symbol representing your topic, or if no visual image comes to mind, write the words. Although you can begin anywhere on the page, it is often easiest to begin in the center, leaving lots of room to record ideas in any direction. For example, if you are making a Mindscape to represent the choices your class has regarding field trips, a central image might be a school bus, a "field trip" sign, or a drawing of children walking.

2. From the central spot on your paper or on the board, freely associate with the topic, branching out in any direction, building your Mindscape to include all the elements you can imagine, using symbols, pictures, shapes, and key words, as well as different colors for different parts of the map. Your first association might be to think about the best time of year for the trips, and you might represent that with a time line across the bottom of the page. Next, if your mind jumps to the historical museum, write that anywhere on the page and connect it to the center with a line. Other possible destinations can be added nearby.

3. Place each new subtopic where it fits in relation to what is already on the Mindscape, connecting ideas with lines and arrows of all sizes, thicknesses, and colors. In this manner, you organize your thoughts as you go.

After you practice Mindscaping on your own, you will be ready to teach it to your students. Perhaps you want to use a Mindscape to brainstorm with your class. Continuing the field trip example, you might begin by asking, "Who has an idea of a picture that will represent the idea of field trips?" You can draw on the board or ask one of the students who likes to draw to do so. Remember that if your own art is not fancy or sophisticated, it will encourage your students to be bold and share their own work more readily.

Coming up with the right symbol is sometimes tricky and may slow down the process at first. When this happens, encourage students to use key words and to add pictures later. Some maps will be primarily words with just a few symbols added. Notice that there are relatively few symbols on the rainbow Mindscape on page 21 and many more drawn on the solar eclipse Mindscape on page 23.

If you prefer to use a template, you and the class could fill in any of the examples on pages 143–154. These encourage you to think through the steps involved in reaching a goal. The template will lead you to questions such as "What are the first steps?" and "What resources are needed?"

You could also create a template for your students. In the case of a field trip, you could draw a school bus on a road and represent your destination with an image or two. Then students can fill in the rest on their own copies. The example on the opposite page is one teacher's field trip Mindscape.

Research and Note Taking

Mindscaping is ideal for research and taking notes, and it is particularly popular for preparing and creating student reports. While reading about a given subject, students can record facts and ideas using words and pictures. As students learn more, they can draw new facts on the Mindscape next to related information. In this way students can organize information while taking notes, instead of taking notes in a linear fashion, then having to organize the ideas later. After they practice mapping while reading, students are ready to map as they listen in class. This requires more skill because they can't control the speed of the information; however, it also engages them in thinking about what they are recording and in placing it where it fits on the map.

For detailed information about Mind Mapping, visual thinking, and the use of graphic maps for learning, as well as dozens of examples, see Margulies, *Mapping Inner Space* (2002).

HISTORICAL MUSEUM

FIELD TRIP

Date:

Our Field Trip

☑ Permission
Slips
Signed

Mom/Dad

Remember: Bring
lunch money

READ | Ch. 9

"World History
on Parade"

Write 3 questions about
Ancient Egypt. Try to find your
answers at the museum.

The final Mindscape can be used for study and review for tests and other assessments. It can also be redrawn to make it more clear and memorable. The process of redrawing alone helps with retention of the information. You might have your students try this fun memory game with Mindscape reports: The students begin by making the Mindscape reports alone or with a partner. After they complete them, they turn their papers over and try to redraw the Mindscape from memory. This activity is not only an engaging challenge, but it also helps the students notice what is most memorable to them. One student might find that she remembers what is in the upper righthand corner, or that she remembers the images she took time to draw. For another student, words or images in purple might be more memorable. Once the students know what helps them remember facts and concepts, they can create more memorable Mindscapes with that in mind. The final work can be turned in as a report or shared with the class as part of a presentation.

The rainbows Mindscape, shown opposite, started with the topic drawn roughly in the center of the page. All the information that pertains to raindrops is recorded above the rainbow image. There is still room left on this map to add more details about prisms, legends, colors, and sunlight, or to add a new branch for an entirely new subtopic. (Remember: If you run out of room on a Mindscape, you can tape your paper onto a larger sheet and continue mapping.)

To make a Mindscape as a final report, students can begin by recording all the information on one big map, then decide what information is important and what is not necessary. Important facts can be highlighted and given numbers to indicate the order of importance. Whatever is not pertinent can be crossed out. The new Mindscape might be made into a landscape with a rainbow, as in the top example on page 22, where the sun and the rain show the right conditions for the rainbow to appear. Other information is added by filling in the landscape. Or the information can be grouped around a central image, as shown in the bottom example on page 22. For this, the student might draw a rainbow and then branch out from there to show the facts in order of importance. Beginning with the one o'clock position and moving clockwise around the central image, the information can be presented in a specific order. This format is very handy for giving oral reports. Moving from "one o'clock," the student can talk about each aspect of the map. There is no need for note cards. The other students can look at the map while listening to the report. Another example of a report created around a central image is the solar eclipse map on page 23. Notice how much the pictures make the information readily accessible. Of course, students can always use their original Mindscapes as the basis for writing a traditional report or for distilling complex information into an outline.

We do not think in a linear, sequential way, yet every body of information that is given to us is given to us in a linear manner . . . we are taught to communicate in a way that is actually constricting our ability to think.

—Richard Saul Wurman, *Information Anxiety*

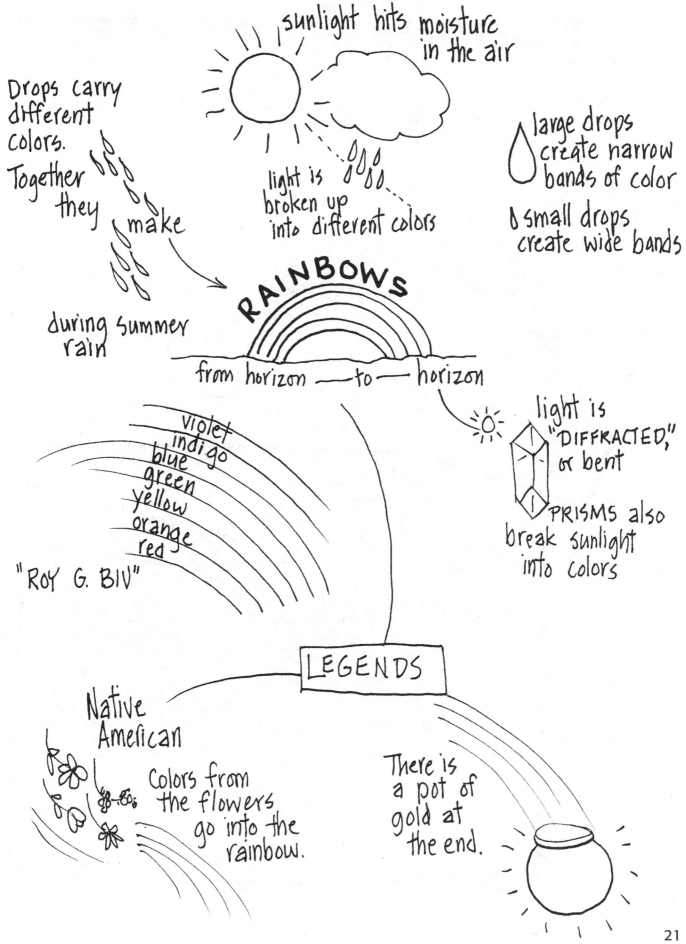

sunlight hits moisture in the air

Drops carry different colors. Together they make

during summer rain

light is broken up into different colors

large drops create narrow bands of color

small drops create wide bands

RAINBOWS

from horizon — to — horizon

violet
indigo
blue
green
yellow
orange
red

"ROY G. BIV"

light is "DIFFRACTED," or bent

PRISMS also break sunlight into colors

LEGENDS

Native American

Colors from the flowers go into the rainbow.

There is a pot of gold at the end.

REDRAWN MINDSCAPES

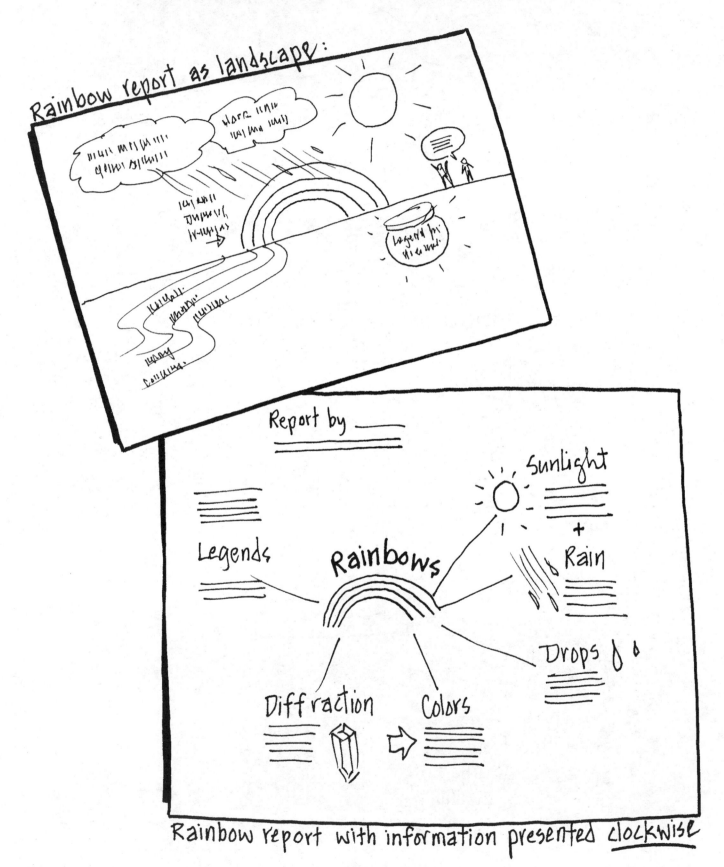

Rainbow report as landscape:

Report by _____

Sunlight + Rain

Legends

Rainbows

Drops

Diffraction ➡ Colors

Rainbow report with information presented <u>clockwise</u>

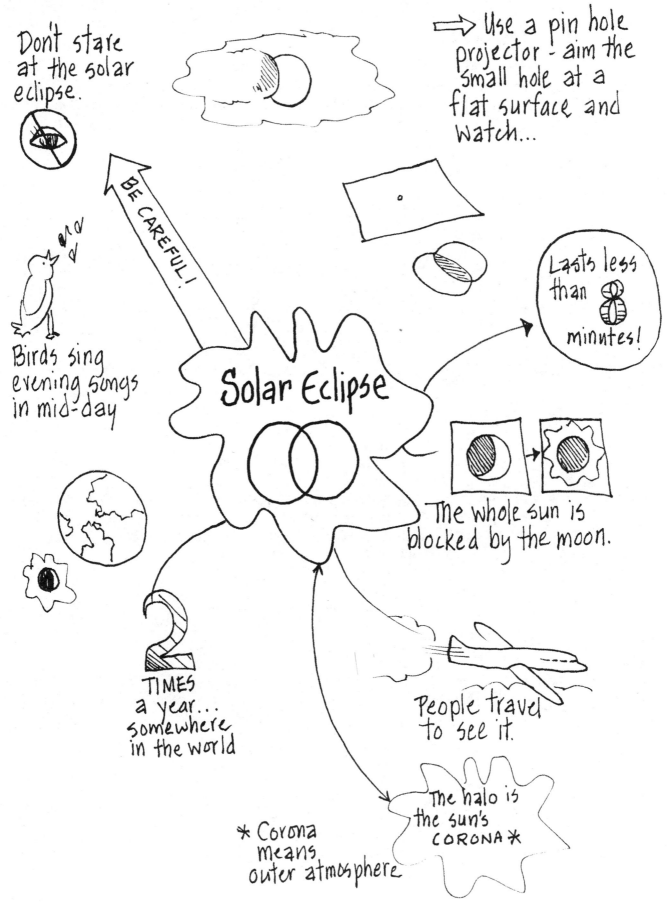

Don't stare at the solar eclipse.

Use a pin hole projector - aim the small hole at a flat surface and watch...

BE CAREFUL!

Birds sing evening songs in mid-day

Solar Eclipse

Lasts less than 8 minutes!

The whole sun is blocked by the moon.

2 TIMES a year... somewhere in the world

People travel to see it.

* Corona means outer atmosphere

The halo is the sun's CORONA *

Outlines

The map opposite is an example of the way complex information can be clustered in an organized fashion. One large symbol represents the topic: Ancient Egypt. Large, bold letters make the subtopics stand out. You can see that there is still room to add more facts to this map. If your students prefer outlines, or you assign them, this map can be the first step, making it easy to then create an outline, like the one below:

ANCIENT EGYPT

I. When
 A. Lasted over 3,000 years
  1. Pre-Dynastic 3500–3100 BCE
  2. Early Dynastic 3100–2700 BCE
  3. Old Kingdom 2700–2200 BCE
  4. Middle Kingdom 2100–1650 BCE
  5. New Kingdom 1650–1100 BCE
  6. Late Period 750–350 BCE

II. Rulers
 A. Pharaoh
  1. Egyptian king
  2. Most powerful person
  3. Made laws
  4. Owned all the land
  5. Collected taxes
  6. Political and religious leader
  7. Declared war

III. Gods and Goddesses
 A. Many, each with a different role
  1. Creation
  2. Floods
  3. Protection
  4. Towns
  5. Plants
  6. Animals
  7. Afterlife

IV. Pyramids
 A. Tombs for the pharaohs and their wives
  1. Many sizes and shapes
  2. 80 pyramids remain today
  3. The Great Pyramid was built for Pharaoh Khufu

V. Daily Life
 A. Revolved around the Nile River
  1. Scribes
  2. Field hands
  3. Farmers
  4. Craftspeople

- Early Dynastic
3100 – 2700 BC

- **WHEN**
Ancient Egyptian civilization lasted over 3000 years

- Old Kingdom
2700 – 2200 BC

- Middle Kingdom
2100 – 1650 BC

- New Kingdom
1650 – 1100 BC

- Pre Dynastic
3500 – 3100 BC

- Late Period
750 – 350 BC

- Made laws

- **RULERS**
A pharaoh is an Egyptian King

- Most powerful person

- Owned all the land

- Political and Religious leader

- Collected TAXES

- Declared war

- Creation

- Floods

- Protection

- Towns

- **GODS and GODDESSES**
Many, each with a different role.

- Afterlife

- Animals

- Plants

Ancient EGYPT

- **DAILY LIFE**
Revolved around the Nile River.

- Scribes

- Field hands

- Craftsmen

- Farmers

- **PYRAMIDS**
Tombs for pharaohs and their wives

- Many shapes and sizes

- 80 pyramids remain today

- The "Great Pyramid" was built for the PHARAOH KHUFU

Chapter 2

The Copy Cat's Guide to Drawing

He who can copy can do.
—Leonardo da Vinci

The notion that some people can draw and others can't is one of the myths of our culture. In fact, learning to draw simple images is easy. It can be accomplished by following the step-by-step methods shown in this chapter, on pages 29–51, and later by simply copying the images shown in the symbolary (starting on page 58). Not only is it OK to copy, copying is central to learning to draw.

Most of drawing is not in the hand, as we assume, but in the mind and eye. You can practice drawing by looking closely and noticing the everyday objects that surround you. As you develop your ability to understand how things look, you will be adding to your capacity to draw. Look at the walls around you. Follow the ceiling line to a corner. Can you see the letter Y created by the corner where the walls meet the lines of the ceiling? If you were drawing this, the line where the walls meet would be exactly parallel to the sides of your sheet of paper.

Imagine someone giving you a sheet of clear paper and a photograph of some buildings. If you laid the plastic on top of the photo, could you trace the lines of the photograph onto the plastic sheet? Most people know that they can trace the outlines of buildings. The next step is to draw the outline of an image without tracing it.

Copying what you see will help you overcome the feeling that you can't draw. If you haven't drawn much since childhood, now is an excellent time to pick up where you left off. Your willingness to be a beginner and share your drawings with the class will serve as a model for giving it a try and not being embarrassed when your work isn't perfect.

I See What You Mean

Drawing is not necessarily about producing a work of art. It is a process that enables us to capture the images, thoughts, plans, and ideas in our heads and externalize them—put them on paper where we can *see* them. It is like creating a projection of the mind onto paper.

As our minds conceive of an idea, most people see an inner image instantly. Our thoughts come and go at a rapid pace. Often we dismiss an idea without really "seeing" it fully. We have such a multitude of ideas that it isn't possible to focus on all that we

have in mind at once; we sometimes get just a glimpse. Once we capture the mind's visualizations, however, we can take a look at them, evaluate them, and see how they fit with other ideas. When the visualization is captured on paper, we can work with it—considering, modifying, expanding, and applying it when appropriate. Drawing will not only invite your students to take a closer look at ideas, it will stimulate their imagination, expand their thinking, and inspire confidence.

You might want to share with your students the habits of such amazing thinkers as Leonardo da Vinci and Albert Einstein. They both used visualization to further their thinking. Einstein saw with his mind's eye the ideas that led to some of his greatest theories. Da Vinci used drawing continually to record his thoughts. Even Lewis and Clark's record of their expedition included drawings as well as words.

Before you and your students try drawing the objects on subsequent pages, practice loosening your grip on your pencil or pen and making some relaxed marks on the page. Try straight lines that you pull across the page (rather than pushing). Let your whole arm relax while you draw ovals and circles. Make the movements rapid and don't worry about the results. Think of these marks on the paper as a record of your movement. Try playing music as students work, encouraging your class to move their arms to various types of music, without pen or pencil at first. After moving your hands over the paper in different rhythms, pick up your pen or pencil and see how the movement shows up as lines and shapes on a page.

The first part of this section groups the objects by shape. It is a fun exercise for students to see how many objects they can draw from a simple square, rectangle, oval, or circle. We have also included pages on depth, size, shadows, contrast, and other tricks of the artist's trade that will make your and your students' drawings even better. Some of these pages will also give you and your students a taste of symbolic drawings, such as how to indicate the passage of time and create global images. Copy and use any of these pages as handouts for students to try in their free time. Each page stands on its own, with instructions on the page itself. As your students are learning the drawing techniques in this chapter, encourage them to start using symbols to take notes. Remind them that they do not need to draw well before starting to do this. The sooner they begin to see the benefits of visual recording, the better. When you and your students are ready, move on to chapter 3 to use your new drawing skills to create symbols for use in your Mindscapes.

Once you and your students gain confidence in representing ideas with images, you can begin to create Mindscapes with fewer words and more visual representations of ideas, patterns, and structures. Students can also develop better thinking skills as they work with Mindscapes that show concepts, map problems, and record steps to solving them. Mindscapes can be used to record students' understanding of whatever topic is being studied.

SQUARES and RECTANGLES

Squares and rectangles are shapes that suggest structure. Try drawing them like this:

CIRCLES

It's easy to draw circles. Relax your hand as you hold your pen. Practice making circular motions above the page until you feel comfortable putting your pen to the page.

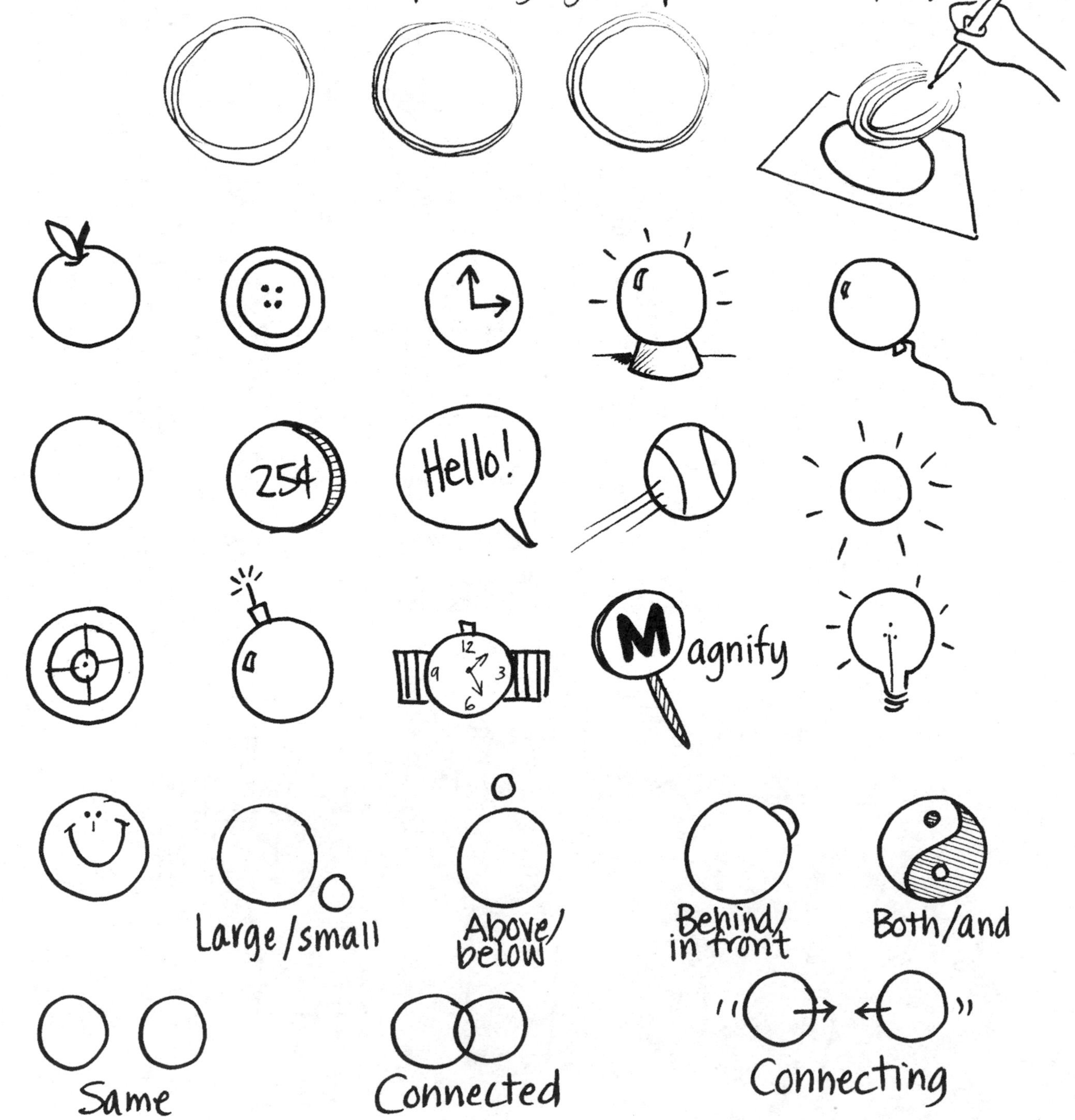

Large/small

Above/below

Behind/in front

Both/and

Same

Connected

Magnify

Hello!

25¢

Connecting

Creativity Challenge: Use each circle to create a different symbol.

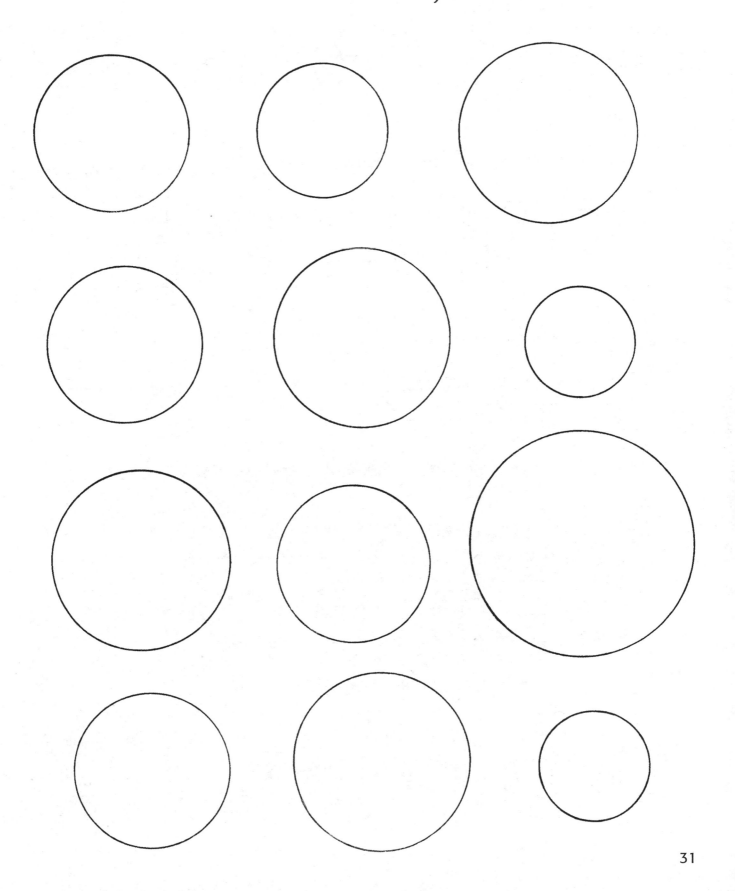

OVALS

But I can only draw ovals...

Ovals vary in shape (thickness) and size.

• Combine ovals and lines... Experiment with shapes.

• Make one of the ovals smaller...

...Erase part of the oval to create a solid shape

• With two ovals, create a coffee mug by erasing the inside part of the bottom oval and adding a handle.

1.   2.   3.

• Your coffee cup can represent:

Full   Empty   Hot   Breaktime   Broken

Remove the handle; it's a flower pot !!

I can draw a
BOX

Package

Gift

Surprise

Building

Factory

WELCOME

This box

Can become a book

Notice the curved lines

ARROWS

Arrows are drawn using combinations of lines and triangles. They can have many uses and meanings. Generally they are used to depict some sort of action.

• Diverge
• Distribute

• Choice
• Confusion

• Growth

• Conflict

• Diversity

• Reverse

• Converge

• Goal

• Blend   • Rotate

• Meet

• Explore

Faces can convey a wide range of EMOTIONS:

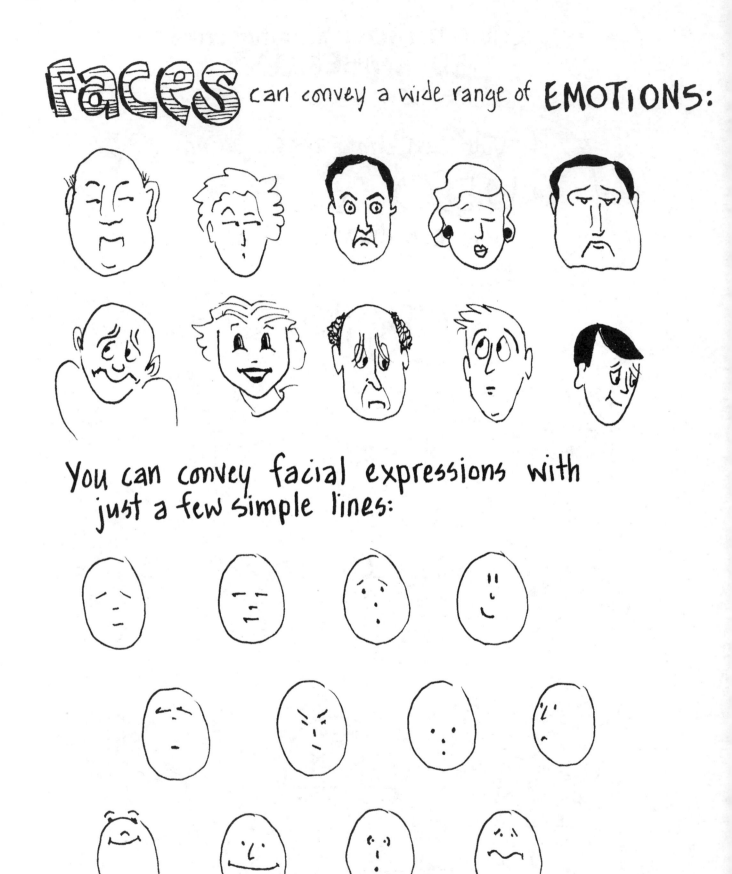

You can convey facial expressions with just a few simple lines:

FACES

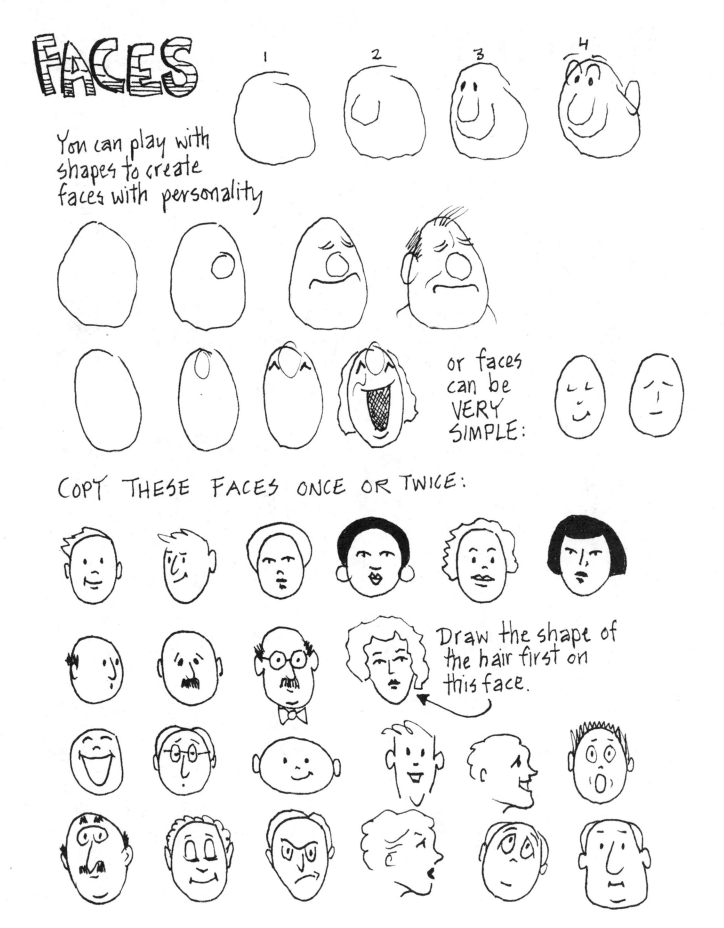

You can play with shapes to create faces with personality

or faces can be VERY SIMPLE:

COPY THESE FACES ONCE OR TWICE:

Draw the shape of the hair first on this face.

PEOPLE can be conveyed with simple figures:

Stick Figures:

Loop Figures:

Star People:

Card People:

Greg's People:

PEOPLE can be drawn using oval shapes:

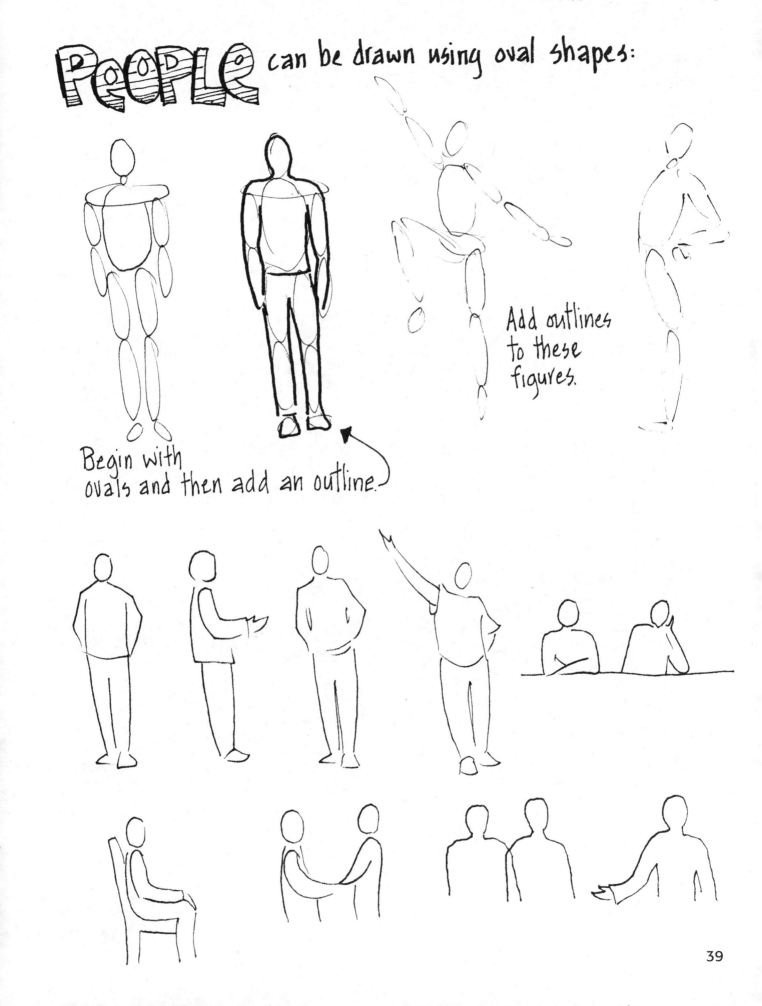

Add outlines to these figures.

Begin with ovals and then add an outline.

HOW TO DRAW COMPLEX SYMBOLS

Take it a step at a time:

Coach

Microscope

CLOWN

MUSCLE

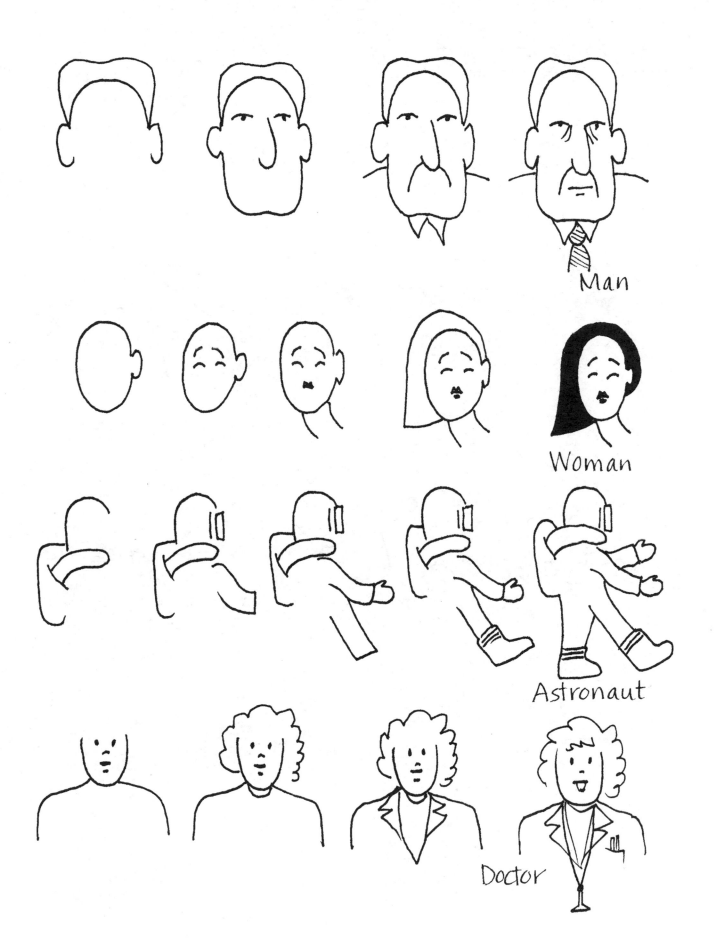

Man

Woman

Astronaut

Doctor

DRAWING Movement

Global
IMAGES

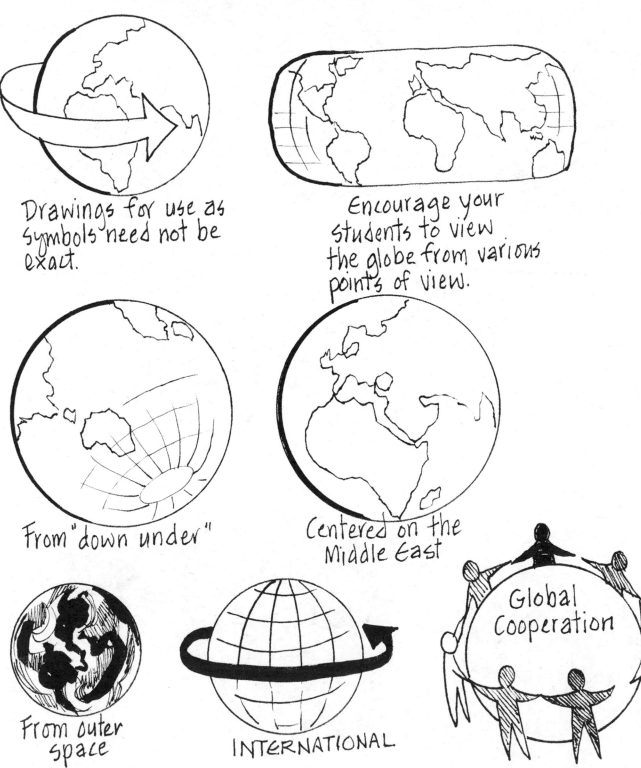

Drawings for use as symbols need not be exact.

Encourage your students to view the globe from various points of view.

From "down under"

Centered on the Middle East

From outer space

INTERNATIONAL

Global Cooperation

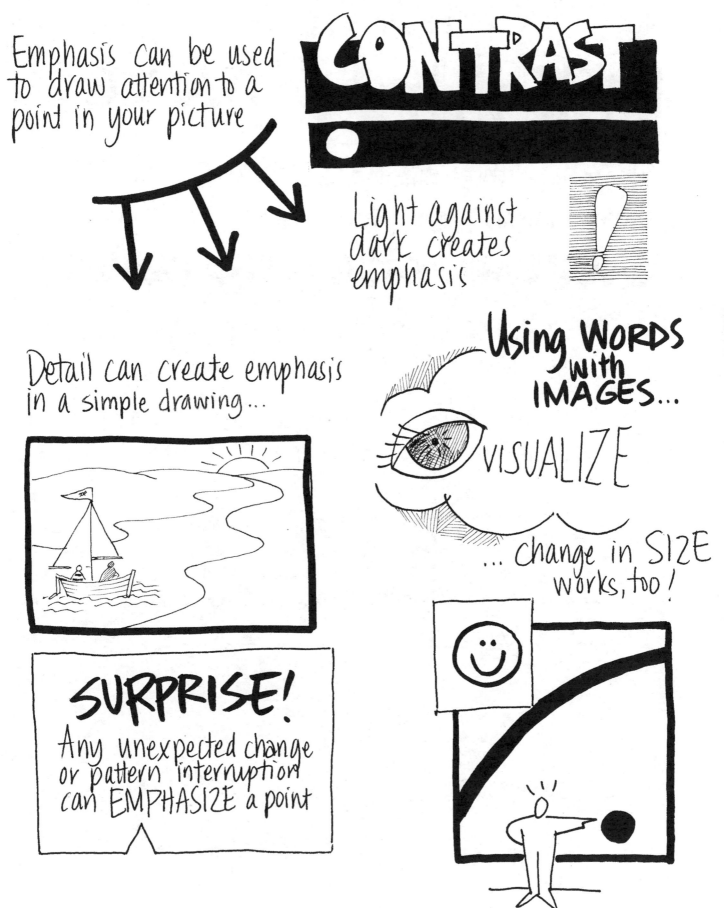

Emphasis can be used to draw attention to a point in your picture

CONTRAST

Light against dark creates emphasis

Detail can create emphasis in a simple drawing...

Using WORDS with IMAGES...

VISUALIZE

... change in SIZE works, too!

SURPRISE!
Any unexpected change or pattern interruption can EMPHASIZE a point

Creating a sense of
DEPTH and DISTANCE

There are three simple things to keep in mind when attempting to show depth and distance

OVERLAP, SIZE and SHADOWS

- Objects drawn in FRONT of other ones make the front object appear closer.

- Generally, larger objects appear closer, except when overlapping.

Adding shading to a surface that is opposite a light source adds the appearance of **DEPTH.**

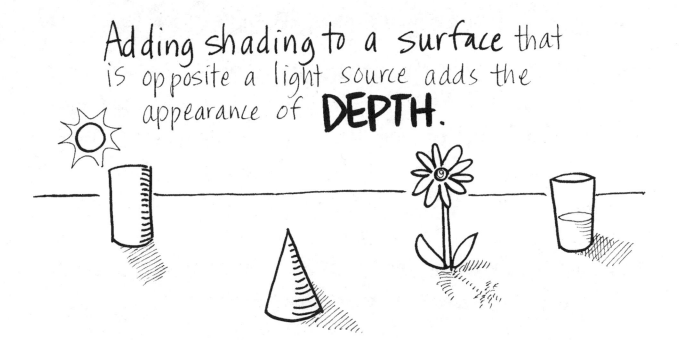

Adding shading or a shadow below an object **ANCHORS** it to the ground...

...or **NOT!**

LETTERS and NUMBERS

The goal of creating Mindscapes is to clearly communicate your thoughts. If your handwriting is hard to read, you may want to practice your lettering. It doesn't need to look like the letters on this page, but if you practice you will surely improve your legibility. You may want to experiment with trying lettering in different sizes, for worksheets and for white/chalk board work. Using a lined sheet as you work will help keep the sizes consistent.

BOLD *ITALIC*

A B C D E F G H I J K L M N O
P Q R S T U V W X Y Z

a b c d e f g h i j k l m n o p q
r s t u v w x y z

1 2 3 4 5 6 7 8 9 0

O O I I I I O O O O I I I I O O O O I I I I O O

C C H H H S S S S H H H H S S S C C

CCCCCCCCCCCCCCCCCCCCCC

—————————————————————

—————————————————————

—————————————————————

—————————————————————

—————————————————————

You may find it useful to do these same exercises with your students.

I I I I I I I I I I I I Ξ I I I Ξ I I I Ξ

/ / / / / / / / \\ \\ / / / A \\ \\ V / / / A \\ \\ \\ \\ \\

I T F T I E T L F T I L T I

Once you feel that your lettering is improving, you might try varying the style of the letters for emphasis. Bolder strokes, larger pens, or different colors can all be used to make something stand out. If you use the templates in this book on large paper for the whole class to see, use a broad-nibbed felt pen for legibility in the classroom.

ABCDEARIUM

An Abcdearium is a sentence containing all the letters of the alphabet. Examples here show handwriting with simple embellishments, easy ways to "dress up" your writing. You might have your students practice their lettering with abcdeariums of their own invention.

The quick brown fox jumps over the lazy dog.

Joy likes watching extra zebras play every Monday under quick fog.

The quick brown fox jumps over the lazy dog.

The anxious Razorbacks won the tournament quite easily after a very good pizza dinner in Japan.

SHADING
and more
SHADING

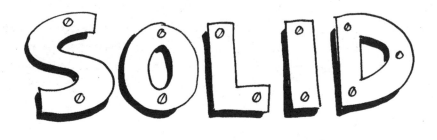

Chapter 3

Creating and Using Symbols

The language of symbols has no words but it can shout warnings, give instructions, direct traffic, and play cards. Without words it can speak in a hundred languages . . . all at once. Almost everyone understands it but no one speaks it.

—Jan Adkins, *Symbols: A Silent Language*

You can introduce symbols to the students while teaching any subject matter. You might start by showing students familiar symbols, such as the ones on the opposite page, or try drawing a number of symbols and asking the students to come up with ideas about what the symbols might represent (see the examples on page 55). Then reverse the process: Write a number of concept words, such as "integrate," "above," or "constitution," on the board and ask the students to come up and draw symbols beneath them. Since there is no right or wrong symbol, no *one* correct answer, students can draw many symbols for each concept. Notice that the same symbol can have numerous meanings. That is why it's important to use words along with images to avoid confusion.

Once you have set the tone by demonstrating symbol drawing, students can create their own images using the symbolary in this chapter for inspiration or drawing upon their own memories and imagination. Let your students know that the root of the word "imagination" is "image." We each have an inner source of visualizing what we want to draw—our own imagination.

Symbols and the Curriculum

Encourage students to use symbols when you introduce a new unit. Give an overview of key terms and challenge students to come up with symbols for each term. You and the class can then use the symbols for taking notes, presenting ideas, and reviewing. You could even request a Mindscape as part of a test. If students have trouble drawing the symbols, encourage them to begin with a word map and add symbols later.

SYMBOLS WE SEE AROUND US

Do you RECOGNIZE them?

pause/still **stop** **rewind** **play** **fast forward**

If the unit is complex and the terms used require background information, ask students to come up with ideas for symbols as you go through the unit. Try the visualization exercise described below.

Visualizing Symbols

We sometimes invite students to close their eyes and pretend that they are in a high-tech screening room. The screen is blank as we enter, but as soon as a word is spoken, an image magically appears. It may change, rotate, or morph into something else. As your students imagine the screening room, read a list of words to them, pausing briefly after each one.

Begin with easy words to visualize:

Book	Love
Flag	Movie
Friends	Ride
Gang	School

Next, challenge students with concepts, allowing more time after reading each word.

Connect	Decline
Imagine	Cooperate
Mastery	Thinking
Mystery	Conflict
Respond	Decision
Support	Equal
Winner	Conflict

(See the symbol examples of some of the above concepts on page 56, created by a seventh-grade class, redrawn by us for this book.)

A challenge for the class ⇨ What could each of these symbols represent? Think of as many ideas as you can for each symbol.

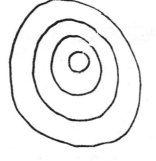

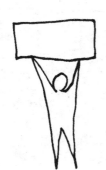

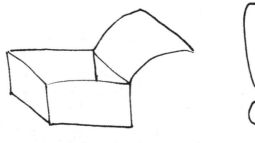

Seventh graders in a science class in California use Mindscaping regularly. We challenged them to come up with symbols... and here's what they created:

DECLINE

INSIDE

COOPERATE

THINKING

CONFLICT

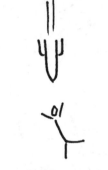

CONFLICT

EQUAL

DECIDE

DECIDE

SCIENCE

Symbolary

Symbols are profound expressions of human nature. They have occurred in all cultures at all times, and from their first appearance in Paleolithic cave paintings they have accompanied the development of civilization. However, symbols are more than just cultural artifacts: in their correct context, they still speak powerfully to us, simultaneously addressing our intellect, emotions and spirit. Their study is the study of humanity itself.

—David Fontana, *The Secret Language of Symbols*

The symbolary in this chapter is designed to inspire your creativity and enable you to present concepts and information to your students in a visual format. After your students have begun to explore visual recording on their own, the symbolary will be a useful reference point for them as well. Begin by looking at the pages of symbols to familiarize yourself with them. You don't have to draw the images exactly as we have. Your own style will emerge. Don't worry about making "mistakes." The goal is to present a simple image that will communicate to your students.

The symbols in the symbolary are a broad starting point. We encourage you to add your own meanings to the existing symbols and to add your own symbols and definitions. As your students become more comfortable creating symbols, encourage them to contribute to a class symbolary, a collection of symbols students draw or find (such as those cut out from magazines or from printed web pages), along with key words that describe each symbol's meaning or meanings. Keep the class symbolary in a binder or have students post their symbols on a bulletin board or wall organized alphabetically or thematically.

Above

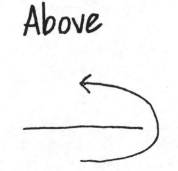

- Advance
- Beyond

Accomplish

- Complete
- List
- Done!

Accountability

- Student
- Volunteer
- Wave

Achievement

- Success
- Excellence
- Good Work!

Acorn

- Future oak
- Potential
- Seed

Acrobat

- Trust
- Teamwork
- Cooperation
- Risk taking

Affection

- Mother, Father
- Baby
- Love

Airplane

- Transportation
- Fly, Flight
- Aviation
- Travel

Alarm Clock

- Morning, Wake up
- Time
- School day

Alignment

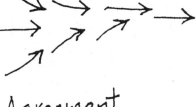

- Agreement
- Cooperation
- Team work

Amazing

- Magical
- Fantastic

Anchor

- Navy
- Slow down
- Stabilize
- Weight

Angel

- Good
- Nice
- Heavenly
- Protection

Anvil

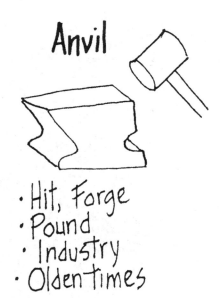

- Hit, Forge
- Pound
- Industry
- Olden times

Apple

- Fruit, Snack
- Computer
- Healthy
...for the teacher

Arm

- Muscle, Strength
- Bully
- Athlete
- Confidence

Art

- Sculpture

Arts

- Paint
- Drama
- Comedy
- Tragedy

Astronaut

- Discovery
- Adventure
- Space Program

Atomic

- War
- Fear
- Destruction
- Weapon

Attraction

- Magnet
- Attracting people
- Force

Award

- Reward
- Trophy
- Recognition
- Winner

Ax

- Chop
- Threat
- Deforestation
- Fear

Baby

- Young
- New
- Brother
- Sister

Backpack

- School
- Homework
- Hiking

Bag

- Lunch
- Container
- Shopping

Balance

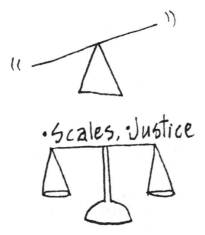

- Scales, Justice

Ball

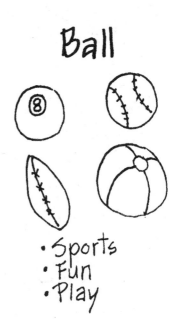

- Sports
- Fun
- Play

Balloon

- Celebrate
- Party
- Float

Banana

- Fruit
- Snack

Bandage

- Ouch!
- Hurt
- Fix
- First Aid

Bank

- Save

Barbed Wire

- War
- Prison
- Barrier

Barrel

- Keg
- Container

Basket

• Picnic

Bed

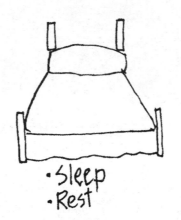

• Sleep
• Rest

Bee

• Sting
• Insect
• Busy

Bell

• School
• Recess
• Ring

Below

• Under
• Around

Bicycle

• Ride

Bird

• Fly
• Migration
• Flock

Blocks

• Toys, child
• Build
• Beginning

Blueprint

• Plan
• Map
• Mission

Boat

- Sail
- Ocean
- Voyage

Bomb

- Explosive
- Danger

Book

- Learn
- Read
- Study
- Journal

Boomerang

- Return
- Australia

Boot

- Winter
- Snow
- Kick

Bottle

- Liquid
- Wine
- Baby
- Formula
- Milk

Boulder

- Obstacle
- Rock
- Geology

Bouquet

- Gift
- Flowers
- Spring

Bow & Arrow

- Archery
- Hunting
- Marksmanship

Box

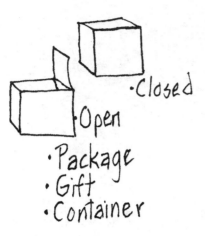

- Closed
- Open
- Package
- Gift
- Container

Brain

- Mind
- Think
- Intelligence

Brick

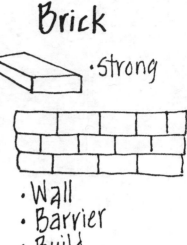

- Strong
- Wall
- Barrier
- Build

Bridge

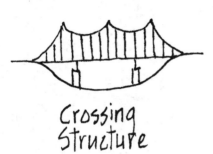

Crossing
Structure

Broom

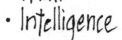
- Sweep
- Clean

Brush

- Paint
- Artist
- Create

Bubbles

- Fun
- Play
- Pop!

Building

- City
- Downtown
- Business
- Apartment

Bull

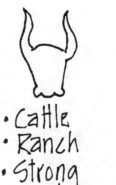

- Cattle
- Ranch
- Strong
- Stock market

Bullet

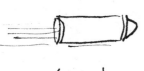

- Speed
- Aim
- Gun
- Danger
- Hunt

Bulletin Board

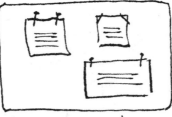

- Announcements
- Flyers
- Assignments
- Display

Bus

- Transportation
- School
- Travel
- Field Trip

Butterfly

- Transformation
- Beauty
- Spring
- Pollination

Button

- Sew
- Fasten

Cage

- Confined
- Protected

Cake

- Bake
- Treat
- Birthday
- Celebrate
- Tradition

Calendar

- Date
- Plans
- Special Occasions

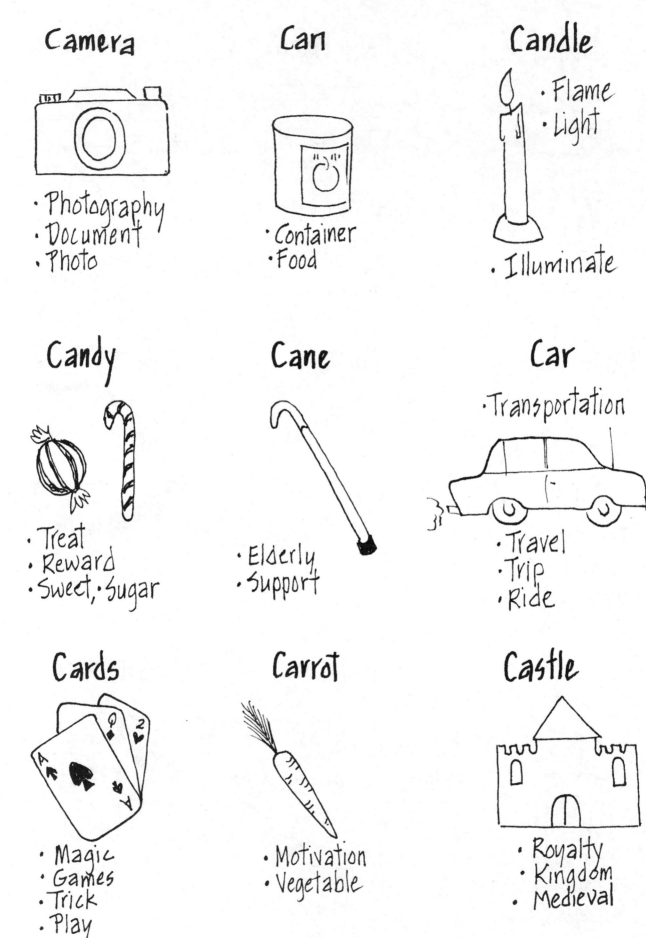

Camera
- Photography
- Document
- Photo

Can
- Container
- Food

Candle
- Flame
- Light
- Illuminate

Candy
- Treat
- Reward
- Sweet, · Sugar

Cane
- Elderly
- Support

Car
- Transportation
- Travel
- Trip
- Ride

Cards
- Magic
- Games
- Trick
- Play

Carrot
- Motivation
- Vegetable

Castle
- Royalty
- Kingdom
- Medieval

Cat

- Pet
- Whiskers

Caution

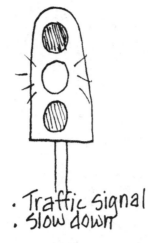

- Traffic signal
- Slow down

Cave drawing

- Primitive
- Early culture

Celebrate

- Party
- Joy

Cell phone

- Connect
- Communicate
- Technology

Chain

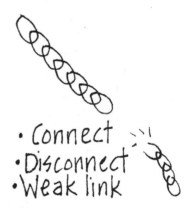

- Connect
- Disconnect
- Weak link

Chair

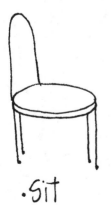

- Sit

Chalkboard

- School
- Student
- Learning
- Explain

Chaos

- Confusion
- Disorder

Cheese

- Dairy

Chess

- Plan
- Strategy
- Game
- Challenge

Chick

- New
- Young
- Hatched

Chicken

- Poultry

Child

- Jump rope
- Play
- Recess

Choices

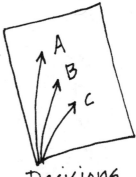

- Decisions
- Options

Clock

- Time
- Overtime
- Time out

Clown

- Circus
- Funny

Club

- Hit
- Bat
- Swing

- Caveman

Coach
- Leader
- Sports

Coffee
- Break
- Mug, Cup
- Soup

Collaborate
- Team work
- Friendship
- Partners

Color
- Art
- Palette
- Artist
- Paint
- Brush

Comb
- Grooming
- Style

Communication
- Announce
- Loud

Community
- Group
- Family
- Neighbors

Compass
- Direction
- North
- Orienteering

Compass
- Design
- Geometry

Competition

- Judge

Computer

- Technology
- Electronics
- E-mail
- Internet
- Research

Concentrate

- Think
- Idea
- Inspiration

Conclusion

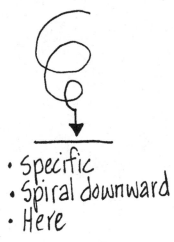

- Specific
- Spiral downward
- Here

Condense

- Pressure
- Conform

Conflict

- Disagree
- Hatred

Connect

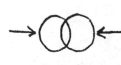

- Inspire
- Join

Consensus

- Agreement
- Conform
- Like-minded

Cooperation

- Team

- Challenge

Cooperation

Cornucopia
- Abundance
- Fruit
- Plenty
- Harvest

Counting
- Abacus
- China
- Unique
- Math
- Addition

Crayon
- Color
- Art

Create
- Make
- Craft
- Sculpt
- Invent

Creature
- Monster
- Frightening
- Nightmare

Crossroads
- Journey
- Direction
- Decision

Crowd
- Class
- Group
- Mob
- Community

Crown
- Royal
- King
- Queen
- Honor

Crystal Ball

- Unknown
- Future
- Fortune
- Prediction

Cut

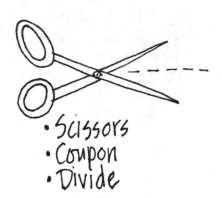

- Scissors
- Coupon
- Divide

Dance

- Rejoice
- Ballet
- Movement

Desk

- Office
- Work
- Study

Dice

- Game
- Luck
- Gamble
- Chance

Dinosaur

- Prehistoric
- Extinct
- Huge

Diploma

- Graduate
- Certificate

Distribute

- Scatter
- Divide

Diversity

- Difference
- Preference

Doctor

- Professional
- Medical
- Check-up

Dog

- Pet
- Faithful

Dolphin

- Marine mammal
- Swim

Done!

- Finished
- Core

Door

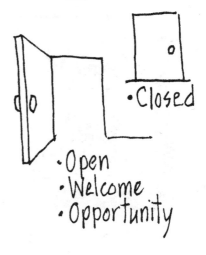

- Closed
- Open
- Welcome
- Opportunity

Dove

- Bird
- Flight
- Peace

Downtown

- Buildings
- Offices
- Apartments

Dragon

- Myth
- Challenge
- Frightening

Drama

- Comedy
- Theater
- Tragedy
- Masks

Drop

- Water
- Rain
- Liquid
- Sweat
- Tears

Drugs
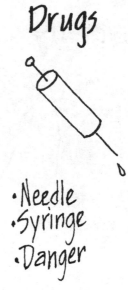
- Needle
- Syringe
- Danger

Eagle

- Endangered species
- United States

Earth
- World
- Globe

- Planet

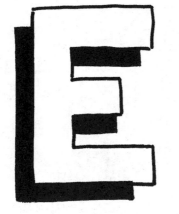

Easel

- Paint
- Display
- Presentation
- Announcement

Education
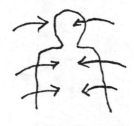
- Learning
- Impact
- Internalize

Egg
- Shell
- Chicken
- Protein
- Birth

Electrical
· Energy
· Plug

Electricity
· Power
· Utility

Elephant
· Memory
· Zoo
· Circus

E-mail
· Connect
· Communicate

Empty
· Lack
· Last
· Gone

Energy
· Burst
· Disappear
· Glow

Envelope
· Packet
· Letter
· Documents

Experiential Learning
I can!
· Hands on
· Doing
· Kinesthetic

Explore
· Map
· Discover
· Territory

Explosion

- Destroy
- Break
- Pow!

Eye

- See
- Watch
- Guard
- Vision
- Visual learning

Fabric

- Cloth
- Curtain
- Cover • Conceal
- Folds

Face to Face

- Meet
- In person
- Connect
- Heart to heart
- Join

Factory

- Manufacture
- Industry
- Work place
- Production

Fan

- Summer heat
- Cool
- Breeze

Fast

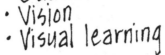

- Speed
- Motion
- Hurried

Feather

- Light
- Quill pen
- Indigenous culture
- Bird

Feelings

- Experience
- Internalize
- Nervous

Female

- Woman
- Girl

File Cabinet

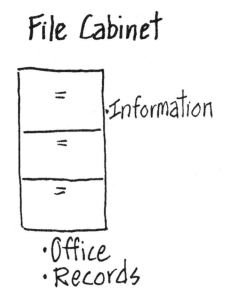

- Information
- Office
- Records

Film

- Movie
- Drama
- Story

Fingers

- Count
- Wave
- Stop!
- Five

Fire

- Camp
- Warmth
- Primitive

Fire cracker

- Dynamite
- Explode

Fire hose

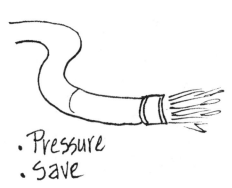

- Pressure
- Save

Fish

- Water
- Ocean
- Marine life
- Aquatic

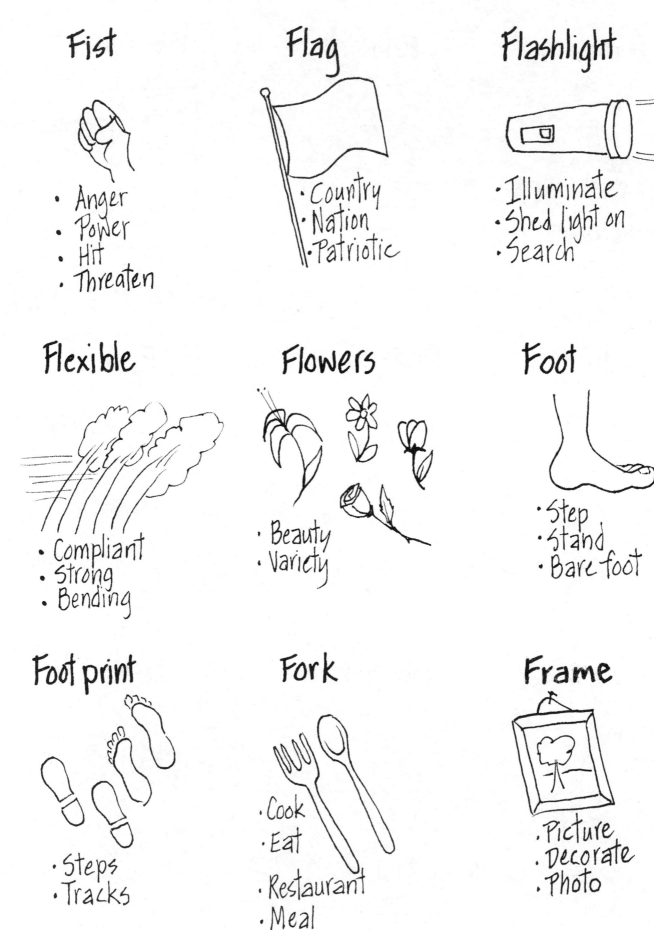

Fist
- Anger
- Power
- Hit
- Threaten

Flag
- Country
- Nation
- Patriotic

Flashlight
- Illuminate
- Shed light on
- Search

Flexible
- Compliant
- Strong
- Bending

Flowers
- Beauty
- Variety

Foot
- Step
- Stand
- Bare foot

Foot print
- Steps
- Tracks

Fork
- Cook
- Eat
- Restaurant
- Meal

Frame
- Picture
- Decorate
- Photo

Freedom

Friends

- Team
- Group

Fruit

- Healthy
- Snack
- Food

Funnel

Future

- Hope
- Dreams
- Goal

Game

- Play
- Fun

Game Boy

- Computer Games
- Challenge
- Compete

Gap

- Challenge
- Missing element
- Fear
- Uncertain

Gear

- Mechanistic

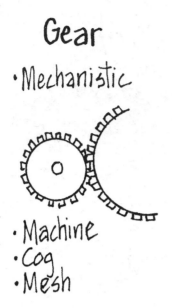

- Machine
- Cog
- Mesh

Gift

- Present
- Surprise

Giraffe

- Animal
- Zoo
- Neck
- Tall

Glass

- Half full
- Liquid
- Drink

Glasses

- Seeing
- Vision
- Perception
- Study

Global

- Community
- Friendship
- Cooperation
- Peace
- Connection

Global

- International
- Countries
- Map

Glove

- Protect
- Cover
- Winter
- Gauntlet

Good Idea

- Insight
- Ah ha!
- Recommended

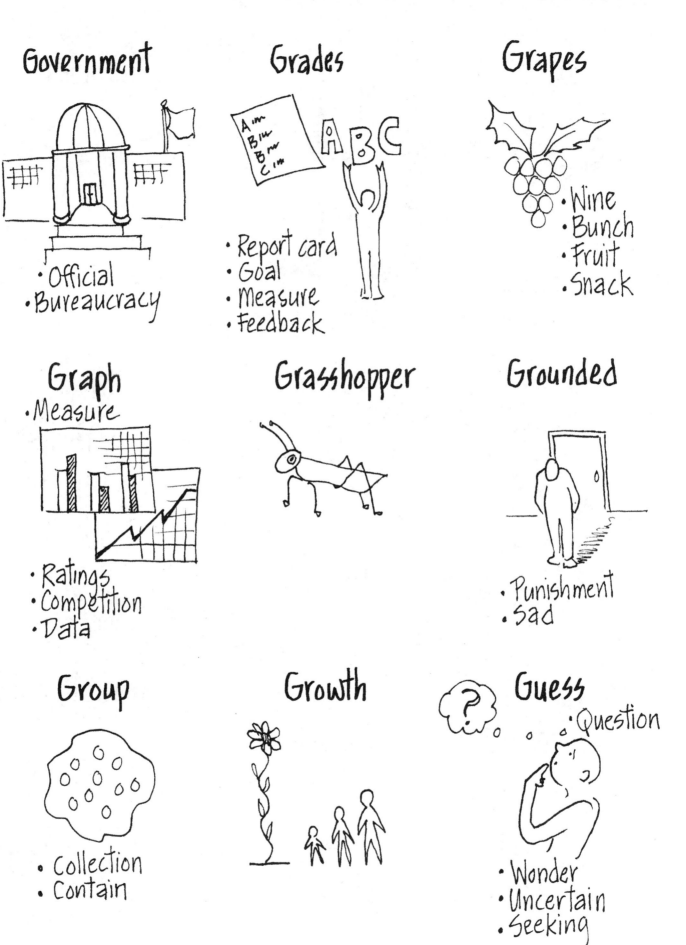

Government
- Official
- Bureaucracy

Grades
- Report card
- Goal
- Measure
- Feedback

Grapes
- Wine
- Bunch
- Fruit
- Snack

Graph
- Measure
- Ratings
- Competition
- Data

Grasshopper

Grounded
- Punishment
- Sad

Group
- Collection
- Contain

Growth

Guess
- Question
- Wonder
- Uncertain
- Seeking

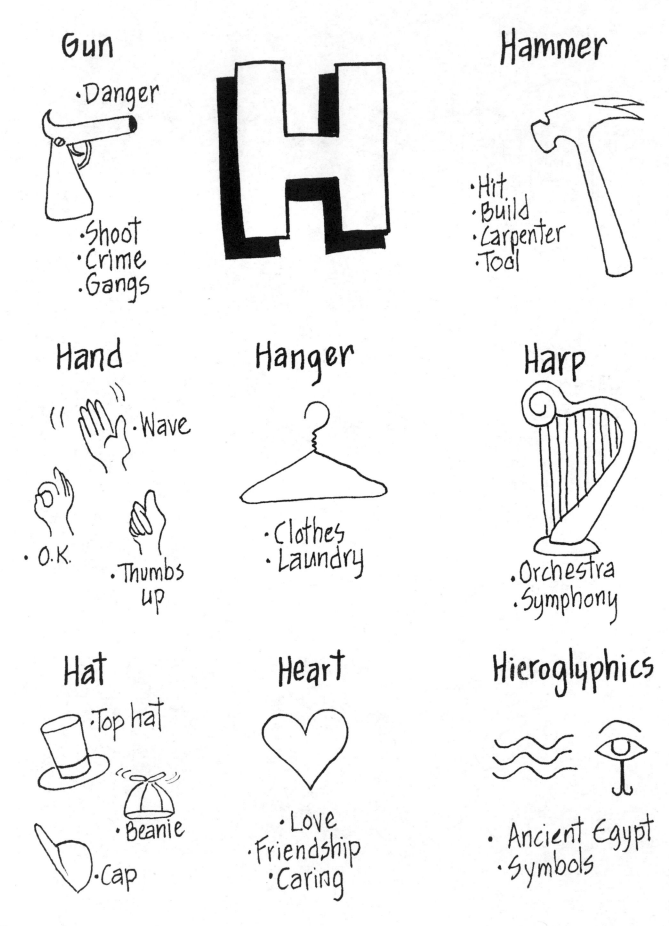

Gun
- Danger
- Shoot
- Crime
- Gangs

Hammer
- Hit
- Build
- Carpenter
- Tool

Hand
- Wave
- O.K.
- Thumbs up

Hanger
- Clothes
- Laundry

Harp
- Orchestra
- Symphony

Hat
- Top hat
- Beanie
- Cap

Heart
- Love
- Friendship
- Caring

Hieroglyphics
- Ancient Egypt
- Symbols

Hole

- Empty
- Unknown
- Danger
- Uncertain

Hook

- Suspend
- Catch

House

- Home
- Neighbor

Humor

- Fun
- Laugh

Ice

- Melt
- Frozen
- Cold

Ice Cream

- Summer
- Treat
- Cold

Ice Skate

- Ice hockey
- Sports
- Glide

Idea

- Creative
- Bright
- Illuminate

Important

- Exclamation
- Emphasis

Improve

- Increase

Incentive

- Motivation

Inclusion

Infinity

- Endless

Inflation

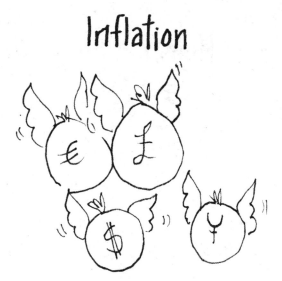

Ink

Inside

Inspiration

- Motivation
- Inspiration
- Intrinsic

Integration

- Combine
- Attraction
- Unity

Isolation

- Left out
- Alone
- Singled out

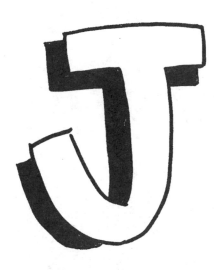

Jackpot

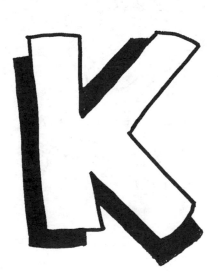

- Winner
- Bonus

Join

- Fit
- Connect

Juggler

- Balance
- Skill

Key

- Answer
- Open
- Lock

Keyhole

- Peek
- Locked
- Open

Kiss

- Lips
- Mouth

Label

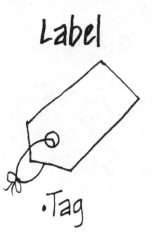

- Tag

Ladder

- Climb

Lamp

- Illumination
- Light

Landscape

- Path
- Road
- Sunset, Sunrise

Lantern

- Light
- Gas
- Camp

Leadership

- Guidance
- Direction
- Mentor

Leaves

- Fall

Lemon

- Sour

Letter

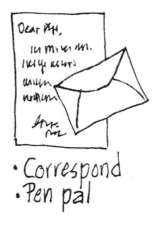

- Correspond
- Pen pal

Lifesaver

- Help!
- Rescue

Light Bulb

- Bright
- Invention
- Shine
- Idea

Light House

- Warning

Lightning

- Storm
- Brainstorm
- Electricity

Lion

- Beast
- Jungle

Lips

- Smile
- Mouth
- Teeth

Listening

- Sound
- Noise

- Hear
- Attend

Lock

· Secure

Love

· Friendship

Luck

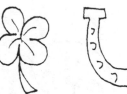

M

Magic

· Illusion
· Trick

Magnet

· Attraction

Magnify

· Research
· Search
· Inspect

Male

· Boy
· Man

Mailbox

· Letter

Map

- Navigate
- Territory
- Chart

Marionette

- Manipulate
- Control

Masks

- Cover
- Disguise
- Incognito

Match

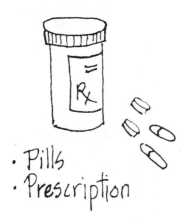

- Fire
- Caution

Math

% # X

+ − ∕ ∶ ∴

> < △

Measure

- Ruler
- Height

Medicine

- Pills
- Prescription

Meditation

- Relaxation
- Contemplate

Melon

- Picnic
- Summer
- Juicy

Memorize

- Input
- Influence
- Learn

Memory

- Elephant

- Remember

Menu

- Order
- Choices
- Restaurant

Microphone

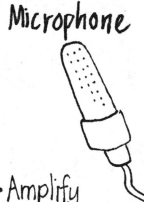

- Amplify
- Record

Microscope

- Inspect
- Science
- Research

Mirror

- Reflection

Mitten

- Winter
- Cold day
- Warm

Molecule

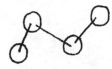

- Structure
- Connection

Money

- Financial
- Income
- Expense

Moon

- Night
- Evening

Mother

- Father
- Group
- Family

Mountains

- Landscape
- Trek
- High

Mouse Trap

- Invention
- Danger

Music

- Band
- Tunes

Music Stand

- Conduct
- Score

Musical Instrument

- Play
- Band
- Song

Nail

- Screw
- Fastener
- Tack

Needle

- Sew
- Thread
- Mend

Net

- Catch
- Collect

Network

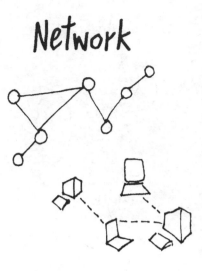

Newspaper

HEADLINE NEWS

- News
- Current events

Night

No

- Prohibited
- Not allowed

Nonconformity

Notebook

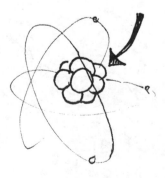

- Record
- Homework
- Journal
- Notes

Nucleus

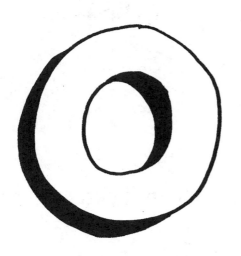

Octopus

- Ocean life
- Many hands

Olive

- Mediterranean
- Snack

Olympics

- Athletics
- Competition
- Sports

Opportunity

- Welcome
- Surprise
- Vanish

Order

- Random

Organize

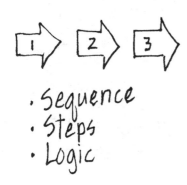

- Sequence
- Steps
- Logic

Outcome

- Impact
- Alternatives

Outreach

- Choices
- Options

Pacifier

- Baby

Package

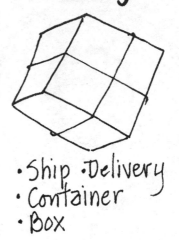

- Ship • Delivery
- Container
- Box

Paint

- Color

Palm

- Oath
- Swear
- Stop!
- Volunteer

Palm Tree

- Vacation
- Island

Paper

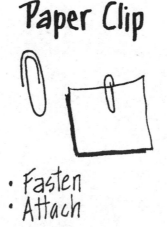

- Data
- Report
- Homework

Paper Clip

- Fasten
- Attach

Paradox

I always lie!

- Contradiction
- Impossibility
- Confusing

Partnership

- Join · Meet
- Agree
- Friends

Party

- Celebrate

Passport

- Travel
- Identification

Patch

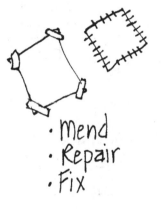

- Mend
- Repair
- Fix

Path

- Road
- Travel
- Journey

Pattern

- Race flag
- Checkered

Peace

Pegasus

- Myth

Pelican

- Bird

Pen
- Write
- Compose
- Draw

Pencil
- Not permanent
- Erasable
- Sketch

Pencil Sharpener

Personal
- Me
- Identity
- Self

Perspective
- Vanishing point
- Horizon

Phone
- Communicate
- Talk
- Connect

Photo
- Image
- Keepsake

Piano
- Keyboard
- Melody
- Song

Pie
- Percentage
- Slice
- Segment
- Portion

Pipe

- Smoking
- Tobacco

Pirate

- Buccaneer
- Looting
- Mean

Pitcher

- Coffee pot
- Pour
- Tea

Plan

- Facilitate
- Teach
- Presentation

Planet

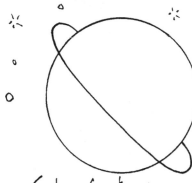

- Solar System
- Outerspace
- Saturn

Point

- This way
- Notice

Portrait

- Painting
- Ancestor

Postmark

LONDON
June 4, 2006
ENGLAND

- Letter
- Travel

Printer

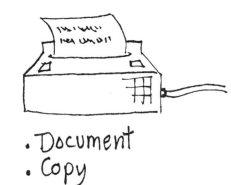

- Document
- Copy

Prison

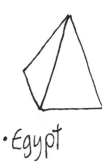

- Confined
- Punishment
- Jail
- Criminal

Problem

- Rainy day
- Doubt
- Concern

Process

- Procedure
- Linear
- Logical

Proximity

- Close
- Community
- Organized

- Alone

Puppet

Puzzled

- Uncertain
- Missing piece

Pyramid

- Egypt

Quantum

- Leap

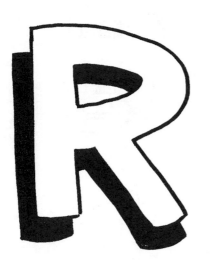

Radar

Radio

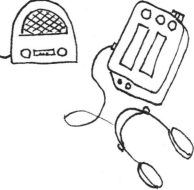

Rain

- Spring
- Shower
- Cloud
- Weather

Rainbow

- Colors
- Pot of gold
- Good luck

Reach ☆

- Aspire
- Inspired
- Desire

Read

- Study
- Book
- Pamphlet

Reality TV

- Program
- Competition

Red Cross

- Medical
- Hospital

Reflection

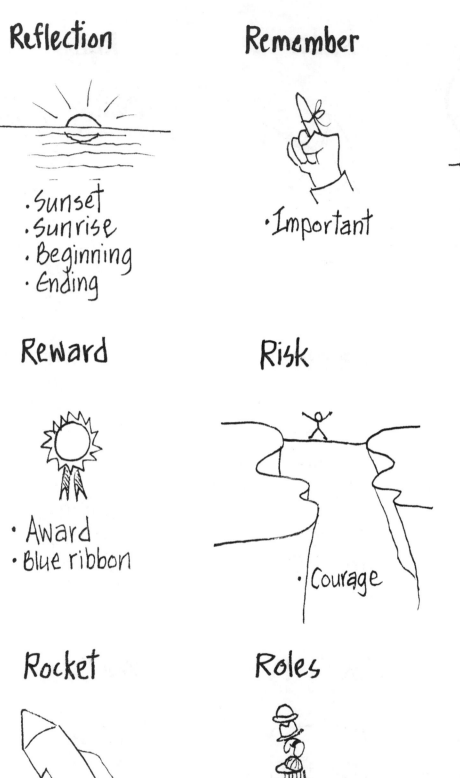

- Sunset
- Sunrise
- Beginning
- Ending

Remember

- Important

Research

- Compute
- Study
- Explore

Reward

- Award
- Blue ribbon

Risk

- Courage

Robot

- Machine

Rocket

Roles

Rollerblade

- Sports
- Skate
- Skill

Rooster

- Dawn
- Morning
- Crow

Rope

- Lifeline
- Hemp

Run

- Race
- Speed

Sack

- Laundry
- Bag
- Supplies

Safety Pin

- Repair
- Quick fix
- Baby

Same

- Different

Same

○ = ○

- Equal
- Identical

Satellite

Save

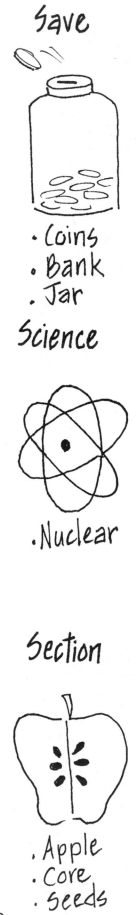

- Coins
- Bank
- Jar

Scales

- Justice
- Balance
- Fair
- Equal

School

- Building
- Community center
- Learning

Science

.Nuclear

Scream

Scream!

- Yell
- Loud
- Fear

Sea Shells

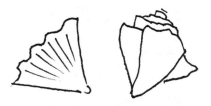

- Ocean
- Beauty

Section

- Apple
- Core
- Seeds

Shadow

- Dark
- Unknown

Shoe

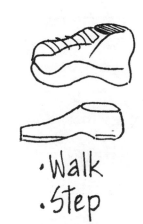

- Walk
- Step

Shopping Cart

· Groceries

Shovel

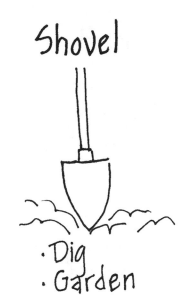

· Dig
· Garden

Sign

· Privacy

Sign Post

· Direction
· Confusion

Size

· Measure

Skateboard

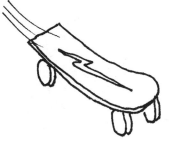

Skull

· Poison
· Danger

Sleep

· Snore
· Night time

Small

· Short   · Tall
          · Large

Smoke

- Cigarette
- Tobacco
- Pollution

Snail

- Slow
- Steady
- Shell

Snake

- Danger
- Temptation

Snowman

- Winter

Space

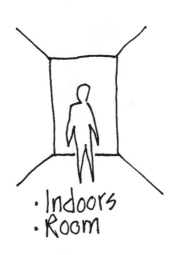

- Indoors
- Room

Space

- Outer
- Inner

Space Exploration

Speech

Hello!

- Talking
- Conversation

Speed

- Fast
- Slow

Spend

Spider

- Insect

Spiral

- Growth
- Creativity
- Unwind

Spot Light

- Illuminate

Stairs

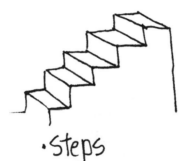

- Steps

Stairs

- Advance
- Climb
- Upward

Stamp

- Mail
- Postage

Stapler

- Fasten
- Clip

Star

- Shining
- Bright
- Wish

Start/Stop

- Fast forward
- Rewind

Stork

- baby
- Delivery
- Myth

Street Signs

- Obey
- Direction

Strength

Structure

- Build

Student

- Answer

Suitcase

- Pack
- Belongings

Sun

- Bright
- Light

Sun Glasses

- Disguise
- Mysterious
- Incognito

Sunny Side Up
- Joyful
- Positive

Super Hero

Support
- Honor
- Assist

Surprise
- Unexpected

Surround
- Encompass
- Group
- Area

Sword
- Fight
- Duel

Synthesis
- Unify
- Combine

Table

Tap

- Faucet
- Water
- Flow

Target

- Goal
- Aim

Tea

- Cup & Saucer
- Relaxation
- Tea time

Tear

- Sad
- Cry

Teddy Bear

- Toy
- Cute
- Cuddly

Telescope

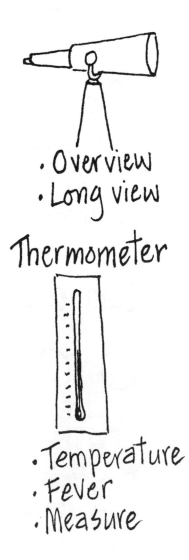

- Overview
- Long view

Tent

- Camping
- Shelter

Test Tube

- Science
- Experiment
- Beaker

Thermometer

- Temperature
- Fever
- Measure

Thinking Outside the Box

Thought

- Dream
- Imagine

Three-Dimensional

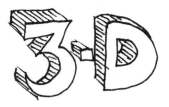

- Dimension

Ticket

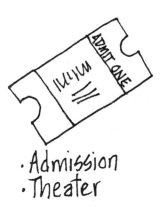

- Admission
- Theater

Tie

- Businessman
- Formal

Time Bomb

Title

- Heading
- Main Idea

Tools

- Repair
- Resources

Toothpaste

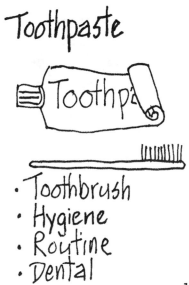

- Toothbrush
- Hygiene
- Routine
- Dental

Torch

- Ongoing

Touch

- Press
- Magic

Toy

- Top
- Spin

Train

- Transportation

Transfer

- Move

Tree

- Forest
- Lumber

Trophy

- Honor
- Winner

Trouble

- Worry
- Bad luck
- Concern

Truck

- Transport
- Haul
- Interstate

Trunk

- Chest
- Storage
- Attic

Trust

- Risk
- Close call

Turban

Turtle

- Slow
- Steady
- Plodding
- Shell

TV

- VCR
- Program
- Entertainment

Umbrella

- Rain
- Protection
- Over all

Uncertain

- Unstable
- Unbalanced

Vacation

· Island
· Remote

Vase

· Container

Virtual

· Invisible

Vision

· Imagine

War

· Tank

Wastebasket

· Throw away
· Trash

Watch

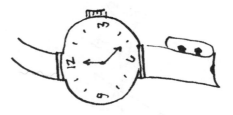

· Time

Wave

· Ocean
· Water

Wave

- Hello
- Good-bye

Wealth

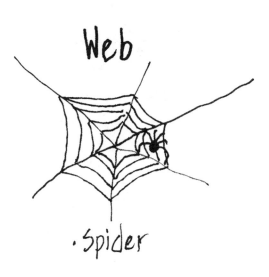

- Money
- Rich
- Abundance

Web

- Spider

Welcome

Whale

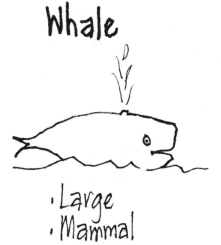

- Large
- Mammal

Wheat

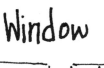

- Grain
- Harvest

Wind

- Breath
- Blow

Windmill

- Air
- Power
- Holland

Window

- View
- Curtain
- Closed

Wings

- Freedom
- Flight

Winners

- Success

Witch

Wonder

- Guess
- Uncertain

Yin/yang

- Opposites
- Harmony

Yo-Yo

- Up & down
- Uncertain

Zipper

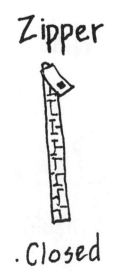

- Closed

Free Clip Art on the World Wide Web

A website of clip art is a symbolary of sorts. Simply looking through a page of clip art will give students ideas that they can apply to their own drawings. Of course, clip art that students discover on various websites can be printed and then literally cut and pasted onto maps they are creating. One way to find clip art resources on the web is to use a search engine (we prefer http://www.google.com) and search for "clip art" or "clipart." Beware, however, that some offers for "free" clip art are not as free as they seem. They will create pop-ups on your screen, or use your information for spam. Here are a few of the most reliable resources we have found. Be sure to read all the information on each site (or included with each CD-ROM) about copyright and use restrictions.

On the sites listed below, you'll find images that can be used in reports, such as the one on Ancient Egypt (see page 25), and in templates, such as the Race Track (page 147). In most cases, you just click on an image to enlarge it. To save it to your hard drive, right-click the image (PC) or click and hold for options (Mac).

The Discovery Channel School's Clip Art Gallery
has a link to a document on how to use clip art in your curriculum. You will also find technical advice about how to save clip art from the Internet onto your hard drive in both Mac and PC platforms, as well as how to insert clip art into Microsoft Word documents. The site also covers copyright and use information. The clip art gallery has sections on health and safety, language arts, letters and numbers, math, music, science, seasons, holidays, social studies, special events, sports, and technology. http://school.discovery.com/clipart/

Graphic Maps
is a mapmaking website with sections designed for use by students, including free clip art of globes, flags, countries, continents, world images, map study guides, and so forth. http://www.graphicmaps.com/clipart.htm

School-Clip-Art
is a site with free clip art for educational uses, with lots of school-related art and other categories. There is also a useful link to other resources for teachers. http://www.school-clip-art.com/

Awesome Clip Art for Kids and Awesome Clip Art for Educators
include many categories of free clip art: aliens, animals, creatures, education, holidays, robots, sports, toys, weather, and more. Both sites also include coloring pages, banners, backgrounds, fonts, icons, lines, worksheets, and wallpaper. They are updated weekly by teenager Tom Brown and his family. http://www.awesomeclipartforkids.com and http://www.awesomeclipartforeducators.com.

Clip Art Packages You Can Purchase Online

Clipart.com

is a subscription-based service with downloadable images. It has images from realistic to cartoon as well as the largest collection of book illustrations in the world (or so they claim!). Images by the masters as well. There are several subscription plans, ranging from a week to a year. http://clipart.com.

The Image Gallery CD-ROM

from the Discovery Channel (http://school.discovery.com/clipart/) is Mac and PC compatible. It is designed for teachers and for students K–12 and is organized by curriculum, with over 3,000 easily scalable images.

Chapter 4
Mindscape Templates

The ability to distil our everyday experience in useful maps and models of the world around us is very down-to-earth: so mundane is it that it is, in many ways, the unsung hero of the cognitive repertoire.

—Guy Claxton, *Hare Brain, Tortoise Mind*

This section of the book includes a number of templates designed for students to fill in or to use as examples for creating their own. You can photocopy from the book and use any template as a handout or, better yet, encourage students to create their own templates, based on the book's templates but larger. Try using flipchart paper or rolls of butcher paper to enable the students to work on as large a scale as possible when working with templates such as the Beliefs Tree (page 163), Aspen Grove (172), and Problem Solving (133).

The templates we've included serve multiple purposes, but we have grouped them according to one of their main functions. The first templates are excellent for teaching and strengthening thinking skills: Circle of Influence (page 123) and Six Thinking Hats (page 128). Next are templates that are ideal for problem solving: Bridging the Gap (page 137), Puzzle Pieces (page 138), Problem Solving (page 133), and Finding Common Ground (page 135). The Book Preview template (page 142) is an effective study aid. Following that are three templates that are ideal for goal setting: Race Track (page 147), Mountain Trek (page 151), and Picture Peace (page 154). The last four templates are excellent for taking a deeper look at our assumptions, feelings, and beliefs: Ladder of Assumptions (page 159), Beliefs Tree (page 163), Tip of the Iceberg (page 167), and Aspen Grove (page 172). The latter templates, of course, also strengthen thinking skills, just as the problem-solving and goal-setting templates do. Choose those that best suit your purpose, and adapt them for other purposes throughout the school year.

Use the templates to motivate and engage students and to teach goal setting and planning, problem solving, conflict resolution, prioritizing, studying and note taking, and how to think critically, deeply, and creatively. They can be used in the classroom and at home and applied to any number of issues from the personal to the global. Many of the templates in this book are similar to those used by global corporations when organizing information for thousands of people to grasp. Visual images often

Try MINDSCAPING your notes about THINKING SKILLS templates here

transcend cultural and linguistic differences. Seeing a plan for the future or looking at how to bridge gaps between the present reality and the desired future is just as useful in business settings as it is in classroom settings. Encourage your students to share their templates with their families and to consider using them to make family plans and to set personal goals in addition to academic goals and other practical classroom applications.

Circle of Influence

Often we are overwhelmed with the desire to make a difference in the world. Yet the fact is we can't affect all the areas that concern us. Author and lecturer Stephen Covey (2004) suggests that we take a look at all that concerns us and then consider our sphere of influence within these concerns. This concept lends itself very well to visual mapping.

For more information about the circles of influence and concern, as well as other principles for setting goals, planning, and determining what is important in our lives, see Covey's *Seven Habits of Highly Effective People: Powerful Lessons in Personal Change* (2004).

1. The large circle is the circle of concern. Here students write about all that they wish to affect in the world. They might desire to stop fighting at school, to help feed the hungry, and to make the world a safer place. Encourage your students to fill in their circles with concerns that are personal as well as global. If needed, provide larger paper so that they can write without restriction.

2. Within the large circle of concern is a small circle that represents our own circle of influence. Within the circle of influence is our own behavior and the attitudes of those around us. Additionally, a student might feel great concern for children living in poverty. This one area can be the focus for the student's efforts. He or she might lead a campaign to raise money, volunteer at a food bank, write to legislators urging more programs for those living in poverty. Clearly, we cannot address all the woes of the world, but we can decide where to use the influence we do have. We can even stretch the circle and do more than we originally suspected.

3. If "children living in poverty" is the area that a student adds to his or her circle of influence, then a loop can be drawn to encompass "children living in poverty" as part of the circle of influence (see the example on page 122).

The important message in this template is that we needn't give up because there is so much in the world that concerns us. By first identifying everything that matters to us, then narrowing that list to those things that are truly important, we can focus our energies and make an impact, rather than being overwhelmed and taking small actions in so many different areas of concern that we end up having little impact. Covey suggests that once you have determined where to place your circle of influence, let go of the rest. Don't waste emotional energy on things you can't change.

CIRCLE of INFLUENCE

◯ = My circle of INFLUENCE

How I act

How I do at school

How much I practice basketball

My grades

Children living
in poverty

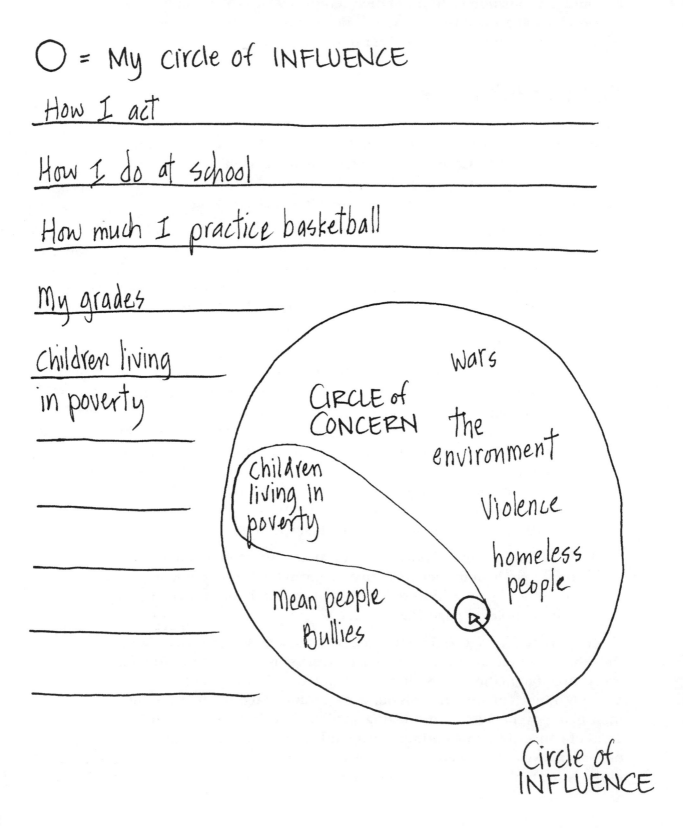

CIRCLE of INFLUENCE

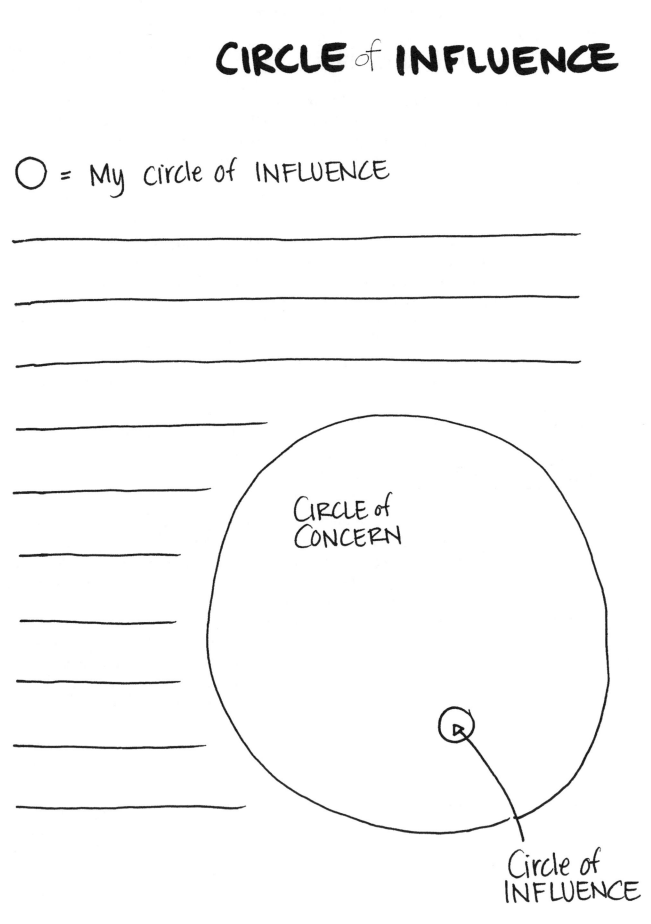

○ = My circle of INFLUENCE

CIRCLE of
CONCERN

Circle of
INFLUENCE

Six Thinking Hats

Edward de Bono is well known for his ability to develop processes that enrich thinking skills. In *Six Thinking Hats,* he points out that one difficulty we often encounter when thinking is confusion. Our emotions and logic and creativity all vie for our attention. When we focus on one thing at a time, however, the whole process becomes less confusing, much easier, and more productive. The Six Thinking Hats system is very straightforward and will enable you and your students to move from confusion to orderly, yet creative, thinking. Your students can imagine that they are wearing different hats for different types of thinking. Using colored construction paper, you and your students can make simple hats to use for these exercises (see the instructions on the opposite page). In some classes, I ask the students to bring baseball hats to school in the colors we need for six hats thinking. The thinking hats are represented on page 128 as a template, which you could copy onto a large sheet of paper or posterboard (24" x 36" works well). Alternatively, you could draw this template on the board or ask your students to draw it for themselves.

You and your students can practice six hats thinking on a wide range of topics. Our emphasis is on using six hats thinking on any problem that confronts the class as a group or is troubling an individual student. As you wear each hat, you focus only on that hat's qualities.

1. Begin by asking someone to state what the problem is. Wearing the white hat, you and your students can examine the facts in an objective manner. Focus on the presentation of pure facts and information. Like a computer, the white hat thinker isn't colored by any particular emotion. Take a few minutes to discuss the question: "Is this really the problem?" Sometimes we go far down the road of solving a problem only to discover that we are addressing the wrong problem. Once you are all clear on the problem, record it in a statement under the white hat on the template. Add any facts that support your problem statement. The example we have included on page 127 focuses on an incident when graffiti was found on the outside wall of the school. The person who wears the white hat might report on when the grafitti was discovered, what it says, and whether or not this has happened before.

2. The blue hat represents being logical and applying the ability to think about your thinking. At any point, you and your students might take a look at your facts through the cool, controlled approach of the blue hat. In our example, the person wearing the

Making a Thinking Hat

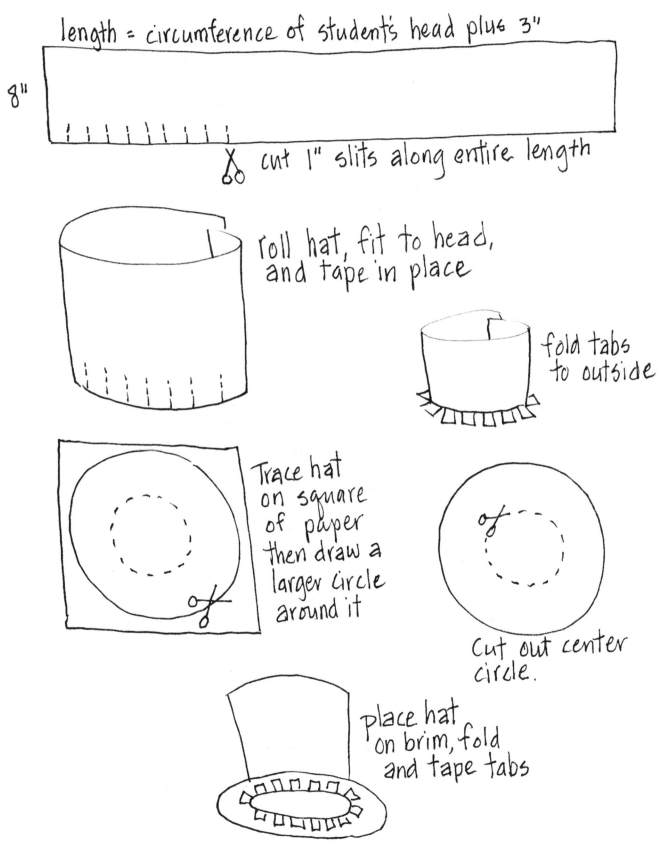

length = circumference of student's head plus 3"

8"

cut 1" slits along entire length

roll hat, fit to head, and tape in place

fold tabs to outside

Trace hat on square of paper then draw a larger circle around it

Cut out center circle.

place hat on brim, fold and tape tabs

blue hat might suggest the next step that needs to be taken. She or he might investigate to learn what the school policy is regarding this form of vandalism.

3. Emotions are signified by the red hat: "What feelings does this problem bring up in you? What intuitive feelings and hunches do you have?" The red hat reminds us that there is an appropriate place for emotions in our thinking. Red hat thoughts can be recorded at any point in the space provided on the template. Wearing the red hat, a student in our example could express anger at the incident or fear that the graffiti is gang related. The question might be asked, "What do you imagine the vandals were feeling that provoked them to write on the school wall?"

4. The world of imagination and creative, fertile ideas is part of green hat thinking. Encourage students to let themselves go and see what ideas show up while wearing a green hat. The green hat discussion in the example on page 127 might involve brainstorming alternative ways to express yourself instead of using graffiti. Students could think of various ways a school could respond to the incident.

5. Any negative feelings, judgments, and ideas about what won't work belong in the space reserved for black hat thinking. Black hat thinking in our example might focus on problems with gangs and the general issue of graffiti and other forms of vandalism.

6. To balance the black hat, try on the yellow hat and take an optimistic look at what is possible. Constructive ideas and opportunities are recorded on the template under the yellow hat. In the example, yellow hat thinking might lead to a decision to dedicate a wall for students to create graffiti as expression. Students might organize a group to go clean the graffiti off the wall or paint over it. Some of the best ideas from the green hat stage could be fleshed out.

7. You and the class may wish to return to the blue hat to review your process and take a final look at what you uncovered during your discussion.

One of the great benefits of introducing six hats thinking to your students is that it gives you a quick and easy method of moving among the various ways of approaching a problem. To a student who is being very emotional, you might suggest wearing the white hat and looking at the facts dispassionately. Perhaps everyone will wear a symbolic green hat while brainstorming, and then move to the cool, controlled blue hat thinking for assessment. It is fun to wear the hats literally while playing out each point of view.

De Bono's book *Six Thinking Hats* (1999) will provide you with many more ideas and a thorough description of each of the hats. We recommend reading it to deepen your understanding of this excellent approach to thinking.

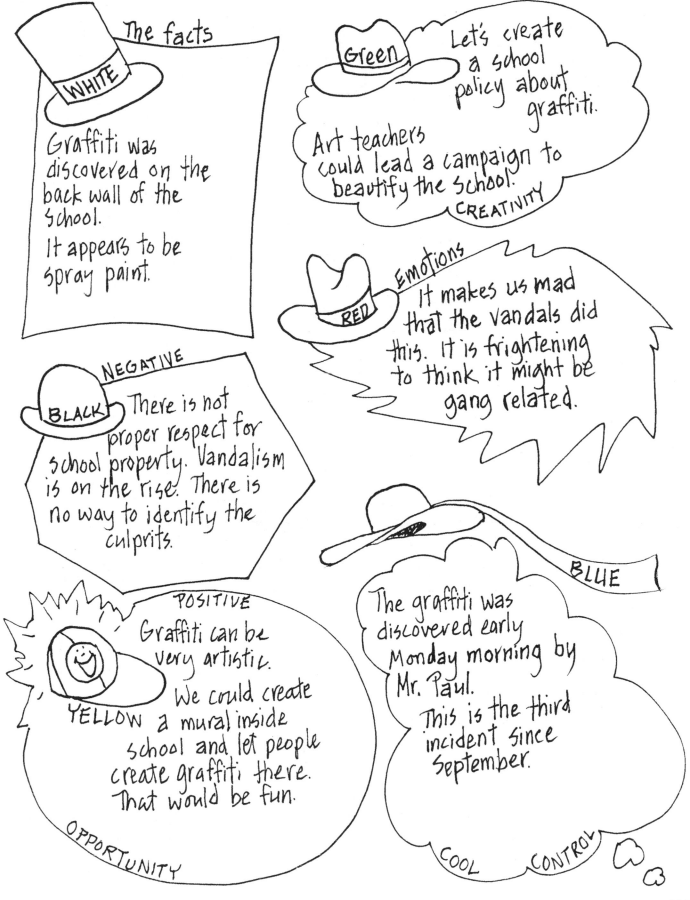

The facts

WHITE

Graffiti was discovered on the back wall of the school.
It appears to be spray paint.

Green

Let's create a school policy about graffiti.

Art teachers could lead a campaign to beautify the school.

CREATIVITY

Emotions

RED

It makes us mad that the vandals did this. It is frightening to think it might be gang related.

NEGATIVE

BLACK

There is not proper respect for school property. Vandalism is on the rise. There is no way to identify the culprits.

BLUE

The graffiti was discovered early Monday morning by Mr. Paul.
This is the third incident since September.

POSITIVE

YELLOW

Graffiti can be very artistic.
We could create a mural inside school and let people create graffiti there. That would be fun.

OPPORTUNITY

COOL   CONTROL

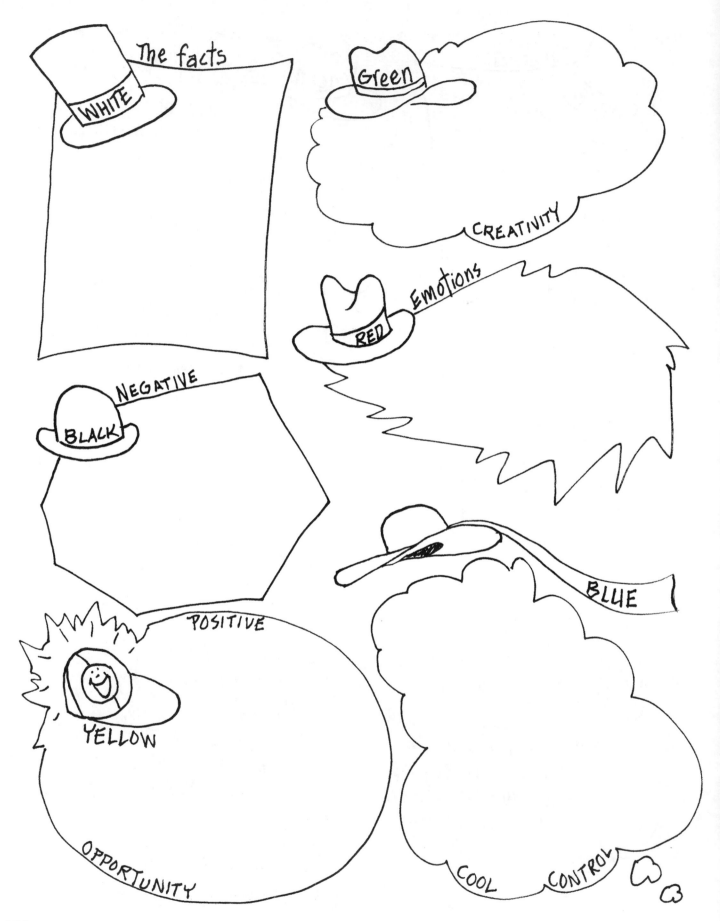

Try MINDSCAPING your notes about PROBLEM SOLVING templates here

Problem Solving

The Mindscape on page 133 is perhaps the most powerful of all the templates in this book. When students begin to approach problem solving with a clear strategy and a sense of their own capacity, they benefit immensely.

1. The first step in the problem-solving template is to state the problem in whatever words the student wishes. Perhaps Molly writes, "I saw Jean copy off Rasheed during the test."

2. Once the problem is stated, the student is challenged to write as many restatements as possible. This might mean looking from various points of view or putting the emphasis in a different place. In the problem restatement Molly could write any of the following:

    "Rasheed didn't know he was being copied," "Did Rasheed know Jean was copying?" "Jean wasn't sure of her answers—getting it right is very important to her," "The teacher told us not to copy," "We are supposed to tell if we see cheating," or "The teacher wants us to know the answers."

3. Next Molly records possible actions. She might remain silent, tell the teacher, approach Rasheed to discuss what she saw, talk to Jean and tell her what she saw, talk to a school counselor, or discuss this with her parents before taking action.

4. For each possible action, the student then records her ideas about possible short- and long-term consequences. Following this trail Molly will discover many things that might happen immediately after she takes action. In one case, Jean will be angry, and the friendship might suffer in the short term. Perhaps Jean will not be angry if Molly just talks to her and doesn't report what she saw.

Although this system can lead to complexity—many possible actions and potential consequences—its value is in the *process* of thinking through each alternative before acting. It is easy to act on impulse and not think ahead of the moment. Many students don't take the long view and consider what might happen in a year or two. Any process that requires thinking before acting has value.

Problem:

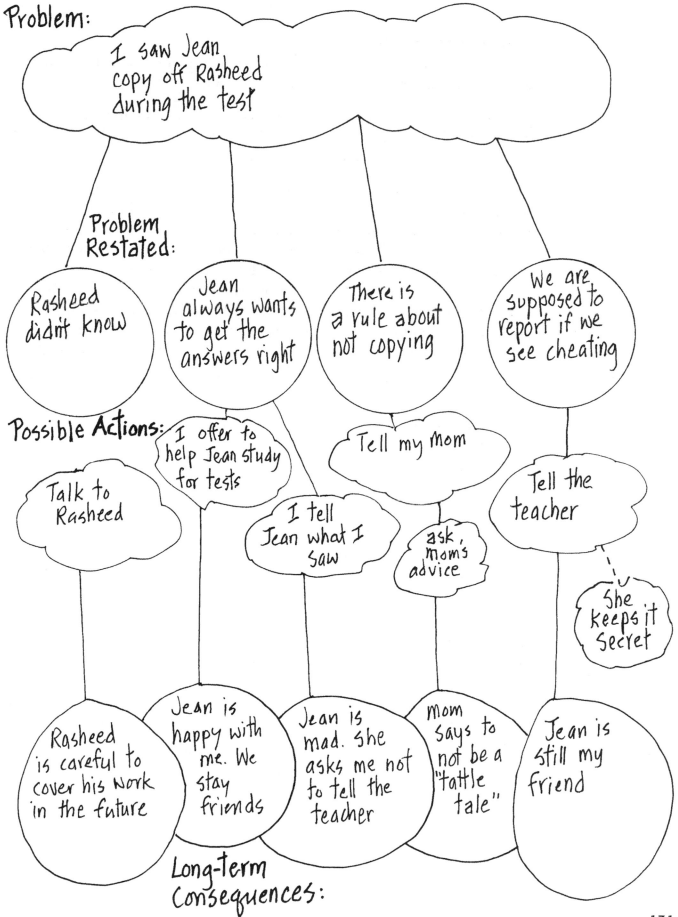

I saw Jean copy off Rasheed during the test

Problem Restated:

Rasheed didn't know

Jean always wants to get the answers right

There is a rule about not copying

We are supposed to report if we see cheating

Possible Actions:

Talk to Rasheed

I offer to help Jean study for tests

I tell Jean what I saw

Tell my mom

ask, mom's advice

Tell the teacher

She keeps it secret

Long-term Consequences:

Rasheed is careful to cover his work in the future

Jean is happy with me. We stay friends

Jean is mad. She asks me not to tell the teacher

mom says to not be a "tattle tale"

Jean is still my friend

Here is another example:

Problem statement: Bill stole a jacket and gave it to Betty. Betty knows this is wrong but accepts the jacket and takes it home.

Ask your class to consider together what Betty's problem statement might be. How would the problem be seen by Bill, by the person the jacket belongs to, by Betty's teacher? What actions might Betty take?

As students gain experience with Problem Solving, they will be able to design their own templates to record the various scenarios. Encourage students to use the template to analyze movies and television, using a problem that arises in the film or show and analyzing other ways the problem could have been resolved. Often, movies and TV present the most dramatic or amusing stories, not the best solutions. Using the template in this way helps students develop problem-solving skills and skills of critical analysis. In the same way, students can analyze how various contemporary and historical figures handled problems and what their options might have been.

Problem:

Problem
Restated:

Possible
Actions:

Use another
sheet of
paper if
necessary

Long-term
Consequences:

Finding Common Ground

The process of mapping lends itself very well to negotiating, or, as we have titled it, Finding Common Ground. When two students disagree, ask them to try the process. It can be applied to conflicts at home as well, as illustrated in the example opposite.

To begin, each person has a large sheet of paper and a few colored markers. (Note: We do not include a template for this particular map because it is most effective if the mappers draw their own from scratch.)

1. Instruct both students to write or draw something in the center of the page that represents the ideal outcome of this conflict.

2. Then each student records all aspects of an ideal final agreement, using one line for each item. When that is complete, the students add to any of the branches anything that they would be willing to do to help resolve the disagreement.

3. After each person has created a map, the two work together to create a third map, one that shows all the areas where they agree and anything either one of them would do to help reach common ground. By working together to record areas of agreement, the focus shifts toward cooperation.

Once students are familiar with Finding Common Ground, they can use it to record both sides of a historical event. They can be challenged to imagine what the two sides might have agreed upon if they had been willing to sit down and talk. In some cases, a historical account includes negotiations and can be translated to the shared map without the need to imagine the outcome.

FINDING COMMON GROUND

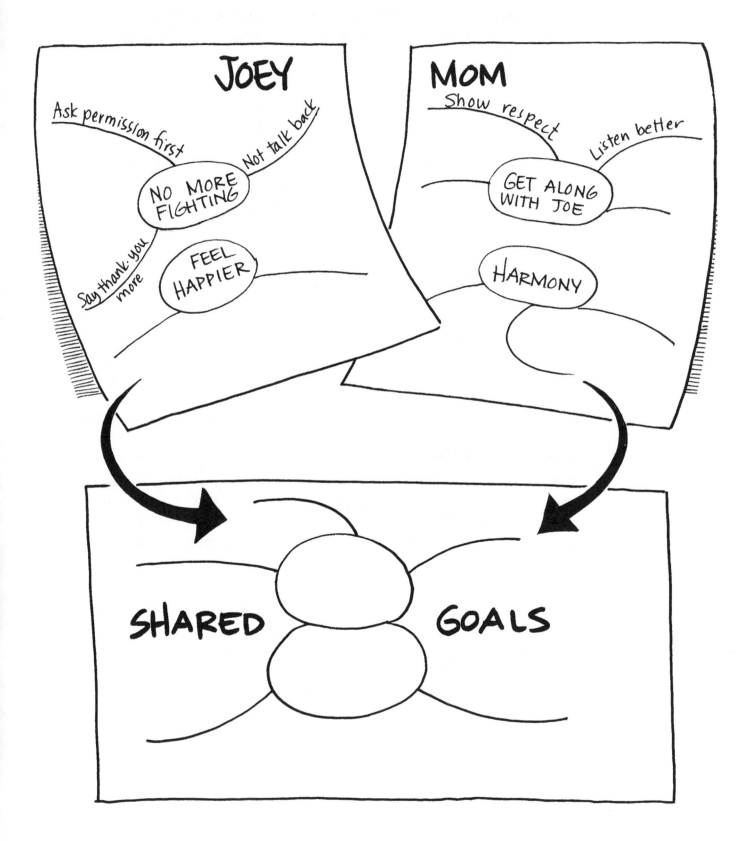

JOEY

Ask permission first

Not talk back

NO MORE FIGHTING

Say thank you more

FEEL HAPPIER

MOM

Show respect

Listen better

GET ALONG WITH JOE

HARMONY

SHARED GOALS

Bridging the Gap

This template provides a clear picture of a situation we often confront: the difference between our current reality and our vision for the future.

1. Ask students to write about their current situation on the left side of the gap, being as specific as possible. A student might write, "My friends tease me," "I feel unpopular when no one asks me sit with them at lunch," "I want to be in a class play," or "I hope to join the soccer team." The current situation might be something from home like, "My parents yell at me" or "I want to feel closer to my brother."

2. Once the current situation is defined, the student uses the cloud and area on the right side to write specific goals or dreams: to stop the teasing, to have more friends, to get along better with parents, to get better grades, and so forth.

3. The challenge of this map is finding the action items or changes in attitude that can bridge the gap between the present and the future. Students can write within the gap or above it. Encourage them to write as many ideas as they can, even ones that seem strange or unrealistic. After writing down all their ideas, they can review the options and highlight those that they can actually put into practice. Another approach to Bridging the Gap is to work in small teams or with another person to brainstorm all the elements of the bridge.

Puzzle Pieces

Sometimes an image as simple as a puzzle piece can spark the imagination. On page 138, part of the puzzle is connected. Students use this space to record what they have already accomplished on a specific project. On the puzzle pieces, they record what remains to be learned, researched, or completed. Students can draw additional pieces as needed.

BRIDGING the GAP

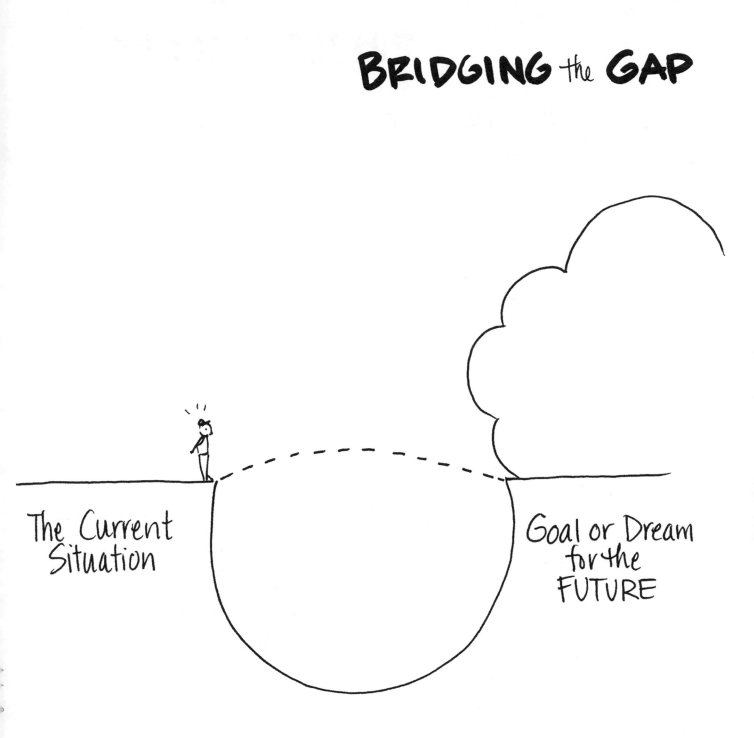

The Current
Situation

Goal or Dream
for the
FUTURE

PUZZLE PIECES

What we
need to
add:

What we KNOW,
or what is already
in place:

Visual Thinking © 2005 Crown House Publishing Company LLC • 877 925 1213 • www.CHPUS.com

Try MINDSCAPING your notes for using templates for STUDY here

study

Book Preview

Prior to reading a book, students can skim it and map the key elements. With this approach, they begin with an overview and are then able to decide which parts of the book they want to read in detail. Book previews usually require large sheets of paper, such 11" X 17" sheets, butcher paper, or flipchart paper.

Walk your students through these steps:

1. Beginning in the center of the page, students draw the cover of the book or a symbol that represents the book. They add the title as well.

2. Next, students skim the book looking for the main ideas only. The clues to main ideas are the table of contents, chapter headings, opening paragraphs, review paragraphs, and the index. Only the main ideas go onto the map for now.

3. After they finish recording the key ideas and main topics, they should read the book and build the map by adding details, page numbers, and quotes.

This template can also be used to prepare a book report, review a book before a test, or prepare to use the book as one of many resources in an essay or research report. A particularly useful technique to aid retention and enhance analytical reading skills is to use the template first to preview a book, then to review the book after reading it. The student can then compare the two, considering the differences and reinforcing the similarities.

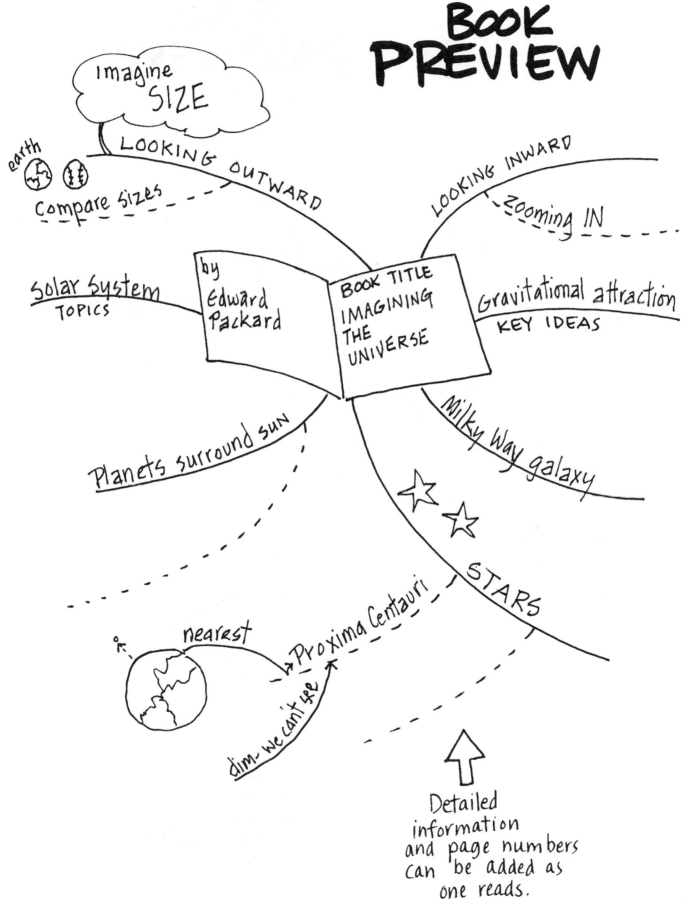

BOOK PREVIEW

Imagine SIZE

LOOKING OUTWARD

earth

Compare sizes

LOOKING INWARD

Zooming IN

Solar System
TOPICS

by
Edward
Packard

BOOK TITLE
IMAGINING
THE
UNIVERSE

Gravitational attraction
KEY IDEAS

Planets surround sun

Milky Way galaxy

STARS

nearest

Proxima Centauri

dim, we can't see

Detailed
information
and page numbers
can be added as
one reads.

TOPICS

BOOK TITLE

KEY IDEAS

Detailed
information
and page numbers
can be added as
one reads.

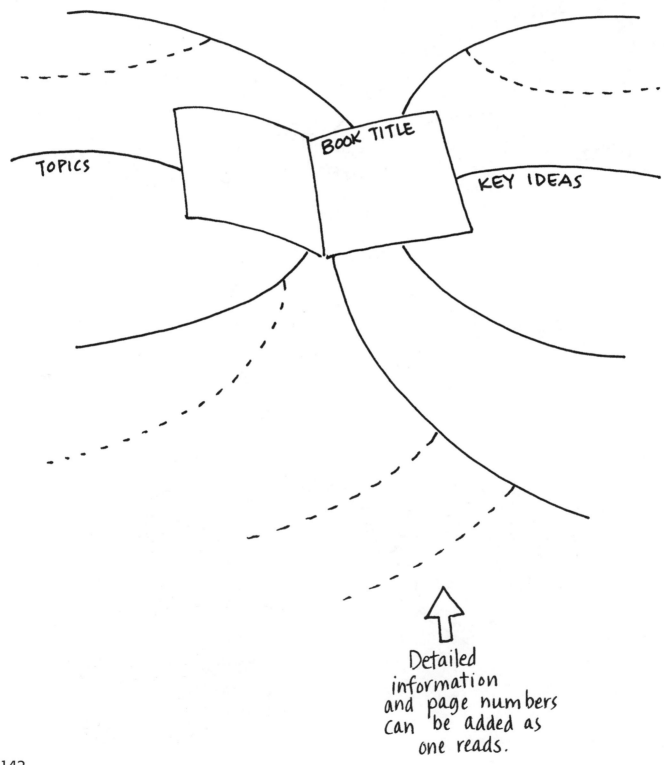

Try MINDSCAPING your notes about
GOAL SETTING templates here

Race Track

Three-time Olympian pentathlete Marilyn King developed the Race Track map with us as a way to encourage students in Oakland schools to think like Olympians. She asked each junior high student she worked with to set a goal and then to fill in the map.

Teaching students to use the Race Track map is an excellent way to encourage them to set goals and then decide for themselves how best to achieve them. In the process they become intrinsically motivated to do what is needed to achieve success. For example, if a student wants to become a professional football player, he may decide that he has to eat healthful foods, get plenty of rest, learn to be a team player, take direction, follow rules, and stay out of trouble. The same student might reject this list if it were presented as a set of demands or even recommendations from parents or teachers.

Imagine this student filling in a Race Track map by drawing a football just over the finish line. Next, he looks at the rest of the map and fills it in in any order he wants. The questions he will need to answer are implicit on the map:

- What are your first steps?
- Who are your cheerleaders? (Who will encourage you in this endeavor?)
- Who will be like a coach to you? (Who will advise you?)
- What will your final steps be? (This might include going to college and playing on a college team, for example.)
- What resources will you need (such as a diploma, money for college, or a scholarship)?
- Who will be like a training partner and run with you? (You can explain that runners often practice with a partner who runs by their side and encourages them to run as fast as they can. Having someone else engaged in the same activity often spurs us to greater heights.)

Try an example map with your students, using a goal that many are likely to have. If you teach high school juniors, for example, you could use the goal of getting a summer job (see the example on the opposite page). Photocopy the template on page 147 for each student to fill in, or fill out one template as a class.

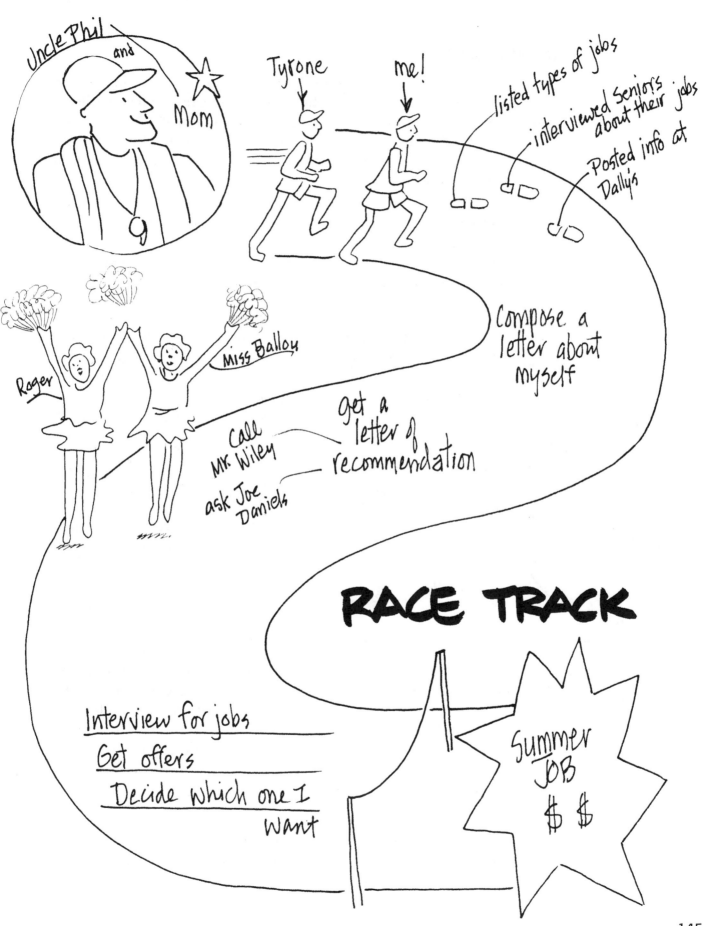

Ideal Image Map

Another way to approach filling in the Race Track map is to begin with what Marilyn King calls the "Ideal Image map." For this activity, students begin with a blank sheet of paper and write down a profession to which they aspire. For example, one student might write "teacher" and another "race car driver." They then draw a circle around the word and add a symbol, if possible. For example, a book and apple could represent "teacher"; a stethoscope could represent "doctor"; and a van with a red cross could represent "medic." Next the students draw lines radiating from the circle in all directions. Notice in the example below (filled in by our aspiring professional football player) that the lines can be curved or T shaped so that all the words written on them are right side up.

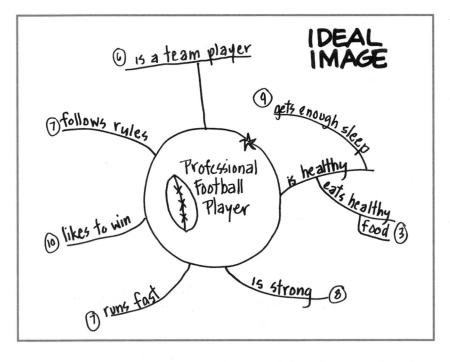

Ask your class, "What are the qualities of a person who is in the profession you chose?" Perhaps the student who chose astronaut would write "healthy, knows about science, respected, brave and adventurous, strong and gets along well with other people." Each word or phrase goes on a separate line.

When that task is completed, ask the students to rate themselves by writing a number from one to ten next to each line they've filled in. Ten means that they already have the quality listed, and one means they need to work hard to acquire the attribute. Now they can fill in the Race Track map by writing each attribute where it fits on the map. The qualities for which they rated high can be recorded on the lines for first steps, since they have been achieved. The ones that they rated low will be steps that happen later on in the race, closer to the finish line. After they record the qualities on the map, students proceed to fill in names for cheerleaders, coach, and so forth.

The Race Track map makes visible the desires of students. After students have filled in the example map, encourage them to use the Race Track map on their own to set specific goals for themselves, small steps on the way to achieving big dreams.

RACE TRACK

Mountain Trek

The Mountain Trek template is an excellent visual method for teaching students how to set goals. As with all the templates, you can photocopy the blank template (page 151) or, better yet, draw your own version on a larger sheet of paper. You can also use the board to demonstrate how the trek map works.

1. Draw the basic mountain shapes and road. Notice that the trail becomes more narrow as it moves into the distance.

2. Ask the students to think of times when they had a goal, something they really wanted to achieve, which met with success. Their first map will be one that records their success and reminds them of how they achieved their goal.

3. Select one success story (such as learning how to roller blade, in the example map opposite) and use that as an example of how to fill in the map. Begin with the cloud. Write the goal there. Use words and, if possible, add an image. If you are stumped, ask the class to think of what image might represent the goal. You can ask a student to draw the image in the cloud.

4. Next move to the bottom of the mountain and ask, "What were your first steps?" Fill in the map accordingly, adding more footprints as needed. Record all the initial activities that led to achieving the goal. In the example, the student borrowed rollerblades, had a friend show her how to use them, and researched used roller blades.

5. Next ask the student whether or not certain supplies or resources were needed. Write these in the bag at the bottom of the page. These might be funding, research materials, or access to a computer. For long-term goals, earning a high school diploma might be one of the resources needed. In our example, the student needed the roller blades.

6. The signposts at the side of the trail are for milestones the student passed while working toward achieving the goal. The first milestone in our example is to buy the roller blades. The second milestone is to practice regularly with a partner.

7. The lines flowing from the boulders are for recording any obstacles the student encountered along the way. You can also ask, "Who helped you achieve your goal?" and write the name or names alongside the trail. In the example, the student felt that fear of falling and not wanting to look stupid were the main obstacles to learning how to roller blade.

THE MOUNTAIN TREK

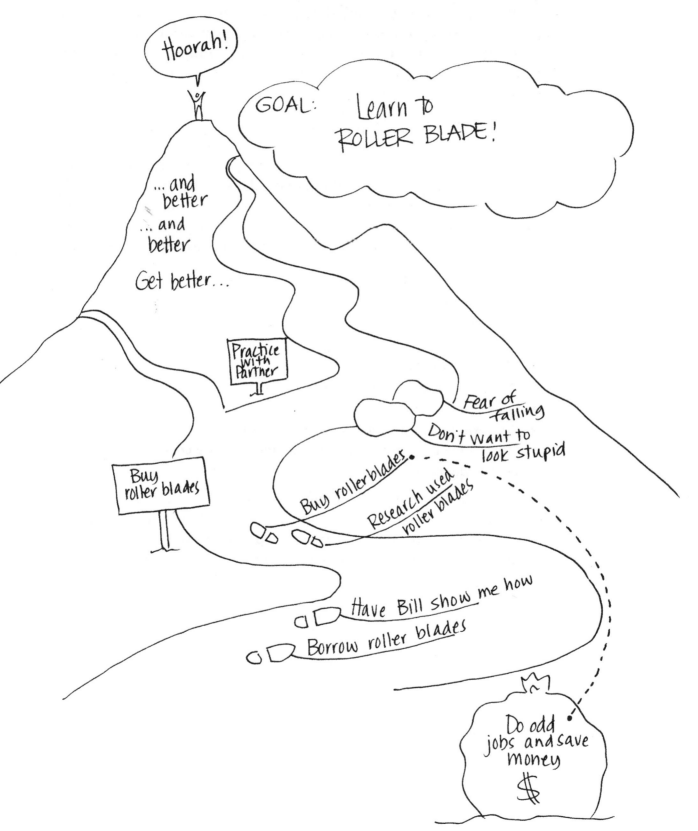

Once a success trek map has been introduced, students can fill in a map recording their own successes. They may need help thinking of an occasion, and you can assist them by reminding them that learning to ride a bike is an example of success, as is learning to swim or play various sports. Copy the map on the opposite page for the students to fill in and talk them through each stage of the map. They should begin with the goal they achieved, and then go to first steps. As you can see on page 149, it is fine to write anywhere on the map. Post the success maps so that students can see each other's work and learn that there are many paths up the mountain.

On another occasion, students can fill in the trek map with a goal they have yet to achieve. In this case, they create plans for how to achieve their goals. The map is used in the same manner as in the success trek map, except that in this case the students are guessing or projecting into the future to discover what will enable them to reach the top of the mountain.

If you wish, post a list of questions to encourage students to think through the trek map elements. Ask,

- What is the first thing you need to do to achieve this goal? (Maybe it is the act of filling in this map!)
- What are your next steps?
- What obstacles do you imagine may be in your way?
- How will you overcome them?
- Who will join or support you in this effort?
- How will you know when you have achieved success?
- How will you celebrate it?

Encourage students to use this template regularly to get in the habit of setting goals. Aside from personal goals, they can use the template to break down assignments, for test preparation, reports, or even entire units (if they have the unit's assignments in advance).

THE MOUNTAIN TREK

GOAL:

Here is a mountain template used for planning in order to reach a goal.

Picture Peace

In order for the world to experience peace, we need to be able to imagine what it would look like in our own lives as well as in the larger world around us. One way to empower your students to work toward peace is to have them fill in the template on page 154.

1. In the cloud, students use words and images to represent one aspect of peace.

2. Next they record one way that they can contribute individually to creating peace. This might be working in harmony with other students, getting along with a sibling at home, or noticing the way they judge themselves harshly and turning that voice into one that is self-accepting and compassionate.

3. In the circle labeled "signs of peace now," students record an event that they witnessed or something from the current news that is a step toward peace. Reading the newspaper or news magazines, one can find many initiatives that lead toward peaceful resolution.

4. Last, the students set a small goal for themselves, recording their next steps. This might involve making friends with someone they fought with, reaching out to make a new friend, or talking with a member of their family in an open and accepting manner.

To learn more about the interpersonal and intrapersonal intelligences, as well as the other six intelligences identified by Howard Gardner, see his *Intelligence Reframed: Multiple Intelligences for the 21st Century* (1999).

These exercises involve the use of our interpersonal and intrapersonal intelligences (Gardner 1999). When we emphasize the choices we make every day, it becomes clear that each student can move toward peace within and peace in his or her relationships. At the same time, the class as a whole can monitor the world for signs of peace.

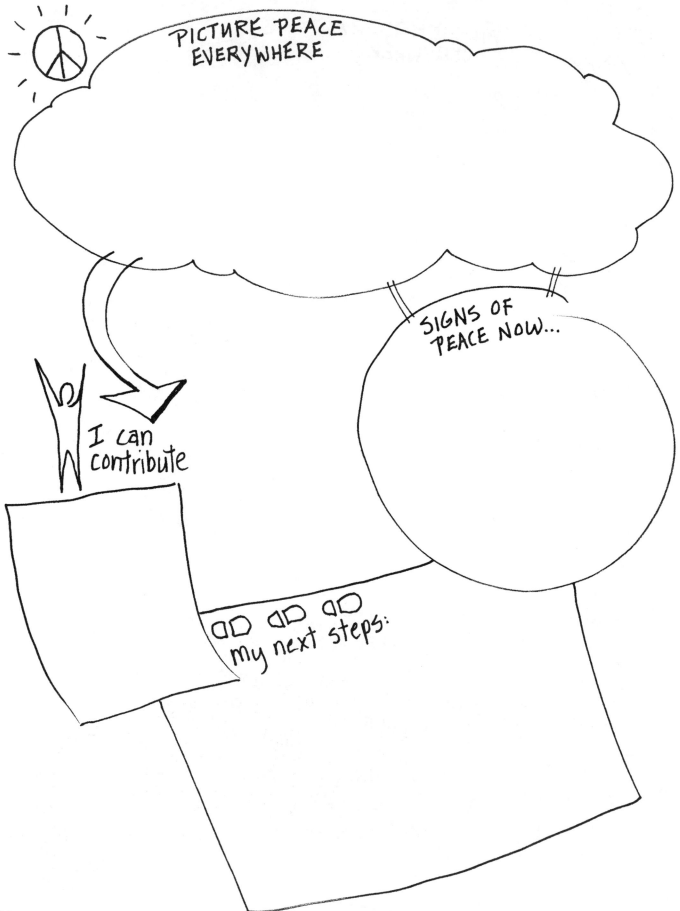

PICTURE PEACE EVERYWHERE

SIGNS OF PEACE NOW...

I can contribute

my next steps:

Try MINDSCAPING your notes for templates to take a DEEPER LOOK here

A Deeper Look

Ladder of Assumptions

The Ladder of Assumptions is an exercise that will enable your students to build their emotional and intrapersonal intelligences. (It was originally designed for businesspeople as the "Ladder of Inference," by Chris Argyris.) The ladder on the opposite page shows you the steps we often take in processing and acting on information.

To explain the ladder to your class, begin by pointing out that we are constantly bombarded by data—little bits of information in the form of our own observations or statements made by others. For example, the way a person acts is data. Noticing that Billy is staring out the window is raw data. Hearing that Susan shoved Renee is also data. The data is not inherently good or bad, it just is. Sandy laughed when Roberto walked past her. That, too, is just a piece of data until we add meaning.

If Sandy laughed as he passed by, Roberto might take a step up the Ladder of Assumptions and add meaning to her action. His meaning might be "Sandy laughed at me." He could let it go at that, but he might make an assumption, such as "Sandy thinks my jacket looks stupid"—one more rung up the ladder. If Roberto continues to climb, he might draw conclusions like "Sandy is a mean person." Before long, Roberto will have formed a belief about Sandy and will view that belief as fact: "Sandy is mean; she laughs at other people. Stay away from her!" At the top of the ladder, Roberto might take action based upon these "truths" about Sandy. He might tell others about her, or he might avoid her or shove her as she walks by, when the reality might be quite different than he assumes. Sandy might have a crush on Roberto and get a case of the giggles when he walks by, or maybe Sandy was laughing at a joke that a friend told her or was simply remembering something that made her laugh out loud.

All of us travel this ladder in our daily lives. In the classroom you will notice many "facts" behind students' actions—facts that were arrived at by climbing the ladder without even noticing the process. The value of understanding this process is that your students can be asked to back down the ladder. Questions such as, "What data is that based upon?" can help clear up many misunderstandings.

Imagine that you attend a faculty meeting and while you are presenting an idea to the group, you notice that Fred has his head down and may even be asleep. You travel the ladder by assuming that Fred is bored with what you are saying. He is not supportive of your idea. He probably doesn't like women all that much, or he's competitive with other men. Fred is not

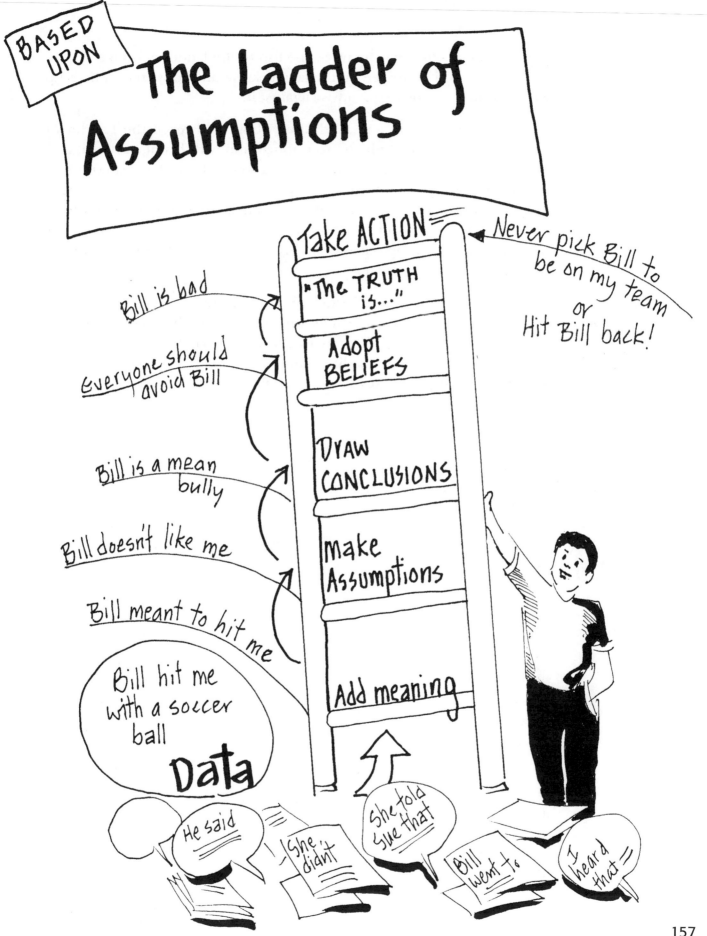

a team player. When you arrive at the top of the ladder and take action, you might let other women on the faculty know all about Fred. If he is up for a promotion, you might advise against it.

Now imagine that you and Fred know about and teach the Ladder of Assumptions to your students. You notice him with his head down, and after the meeting you say, "Fred, I noticed you had your head down when I was making a proposal. Are you opposed to it?" Fred's answer might surprise you. He might reply, "Not at all. I am in favor. It's just that when I concentrate on an issue, I close my eyes and mull it over. I was very interested in your proposal and was giving it my full attention. Count on me when it comes to a vote."

You may wish to copy the ladder on the opposite page as a handout. Students can think of their own examples and fill in the spaces to the left of the ladder. Encourage them to use the ladder to help them understand other people's actions, including family and friends, characters in books and stories, historical figures, and even the actions of entire countries.

Beliefs Tree

It is useful to fill in the Beliefs Tree with your own ideas before introducing it to your class. Begin by deciding what topic you want to explore. For example, if you decide to explore trust, write that word on or near the tree trunk. Next consider your beliefs about trust. Ask yourself, what are my beliefs about trust? Your answers might include "Don't trust strangers," "Don't trust women," or "Don't trust men." On the positive side you might record "Trust people who prove themselves trustworthy" or "Trust must be earned" or "Trust family only."

The Beliefs Tree enables you to record your beliefs on the branches of the tree and the origins of those beliefs in the root system. Once you have recorded ideas about trust in the branches, consider how you came to these beliefs. Feel free to move back and forth between the branches and roots as new ideas occur to you. Remember that every "truism" was once an assumption, and you may now hold beliefs formed years ago. Once you have explored the origin of your beliefs, you can decide if they are still valid or are left over notions that, once surfaced, you realize are not true. The roots of your beliefs may include what you were told as a child, what you experienced once in the distant past, or recent events that may reinforce your beliefs.

Encourage your students to explore what they hold as true about a given topic. You might select topics such as trust, truth, consequences, fairness, girls, boys, men, women, school, learning, intelligence, drugs, or gangs.

1. When introducing the tree to your class, begin with a large tree on the board, similar to the one on page 163. You can also photocopy the tree and distribute it to the class.

2. Walk the students through one example of the tree, eliciting ideas from them about both beliefs and their origins. You can read a story to the class or refer to one they are reading and guess what the beliefs and origins of beliefs are of one of the characters. Or use the tree to discuss political beliefs associated with historical or current events, or to discuss a scientific experiment before trying it, with students writing what they hypothesize will happen in the branches and why they believe these things will happen in the roots (or they could fill in the roots after the experiment is conducted).

The tree is named "the Beliefs Tree," because it will encourage you and your students to think about how often we decide something is "true" without realizing that we made an assumption at some point in our lives and then held that opinion as carved in stone. The ladder template (page 159) provides another opportunity for students to explore how we jump to conclusions and hold on to "truths" that are in fact just hastily determined or outdated beliefs.

THE BELIEFS TREE

I'm supposed to believe my teacher

People don't trust me

Don't trust strangers

TOPIC:

Trust

Filling in this tree and its root system enables students to explore their assumptions and the root of various beliefs.

ORIGIN OF BELIEFS:

You have to earn trust

I promise stuff I don't do

One time Dad said he would visit, but he didn't

Mom told me never to trust strangers

Adults know what is best

THE BELIEFS TREE

TOPIC:

Filling in this tree and its root system enables students to explore their assumptions and the root of various beliefs.

ORIGIN OF BELIEFS:

Tip of the Iceberg

The Tip of the Iceberg enables students to consider that what is obvious to them may be a small part of a larger story. Looking below the surface for what is hidden challenges the student to think deeply.

In our example (on page 166) what is obvious is that a student, call her Sharon, is not doing well in school. One of the contributing factors is that her parents are fighting. Sharon is afraid her parents might get a divorce. In fact, the "shark in the waters" for Sharon is the idea of divorce. Near the small boat Sharon can record the people or resources that might assist her in addressing her problem.

Deep in the bedrock of the ocean, basic assumptions that seem to be truths for Sharon can be recorded. She may believe that she can't talk to her parents, that she is a poor student, that she misses sleep simply because she likes to stay up late. The value in filling in the Tip of the Iceberg template is that Sharon can now look at the big picture. She can consider a number of factors that may lead to her poor grades. Of equal importance is that Sharon can question her deeply held assumptions. This may lead to her talking to one or both of her parents to express her concerns. Or she might recall that in many instances she has been a good student.

This template can be applied to historical events so that students understand that a single event cannot be fully understood without considering the context, influences, and climate of the time. Looking for the deeper "truths" encourages students to question their beliefs, understand the assumptions of others, and develop critical-thinking skills.

THE **TIP** of the **ICEBERG**

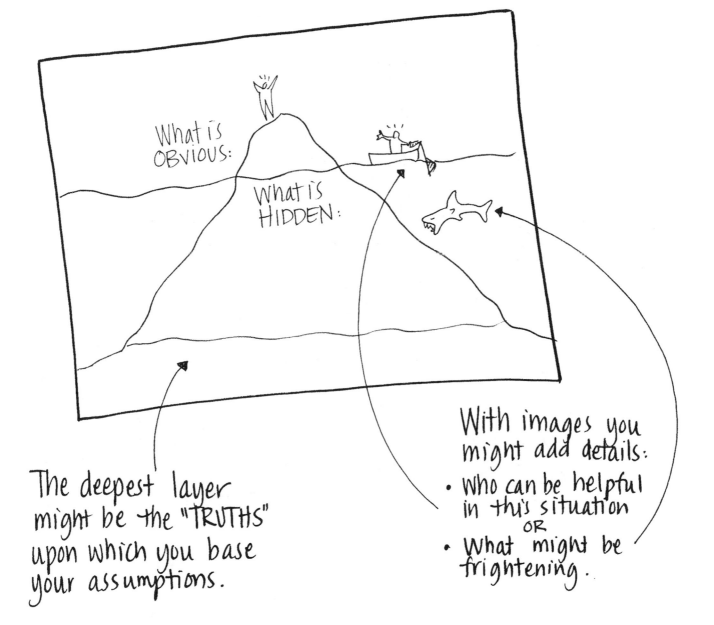

What is OBVIOUS:

What is HIDDEN:

The deepest layer might be the "TRUTHS" upon which you base your assumptions.

With images you might add details:
• Who can be helpful in this situation
  OR
• What might be frightening.

The Tip of the Iceberg template can be used to show what is KNOWN and NOT KNOWN about a situation, person, or thing. Or to explore what is obvious and what is hidden.

TIP of the ICEBERG

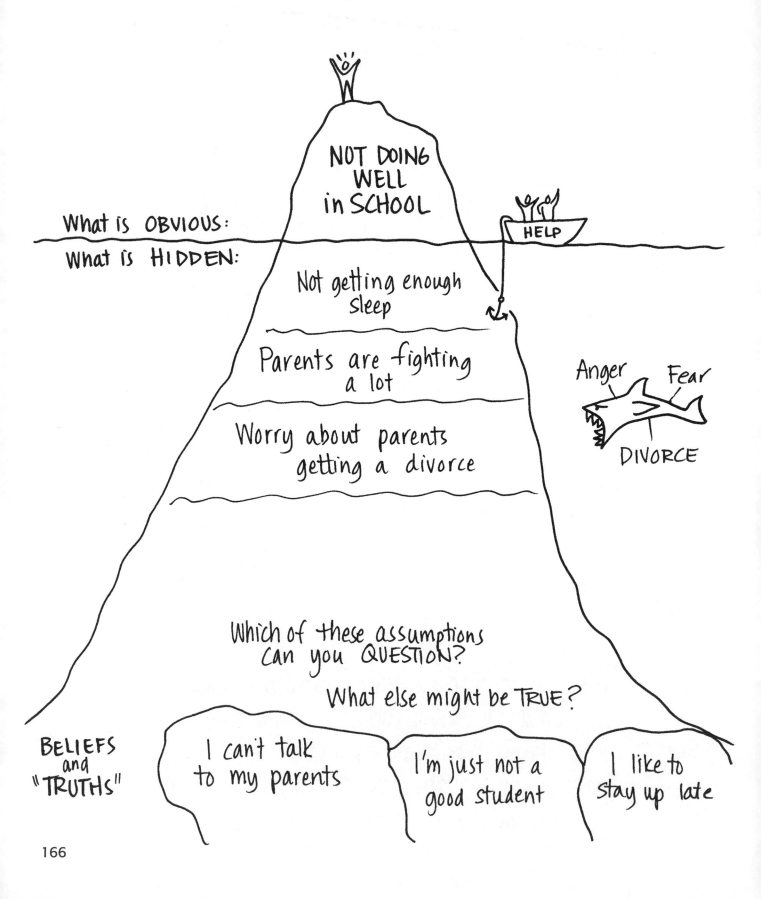

NOT DOING WELL in SCHOOL

What is OBVIOUS:

What is HIDDEN:

Not getting enough sleep

HELP

Parents are fighting a lot

Worry about parents getting a divorce

Anger   Fear

DIVORCE

Which of these assumptions can you QUESTION?

What else might be TRUE?

BELIEFS and "TRUTHS"

I can't talk to my parents

I'm just not a good student

I like to stay up late

TIP of the ICEBERG

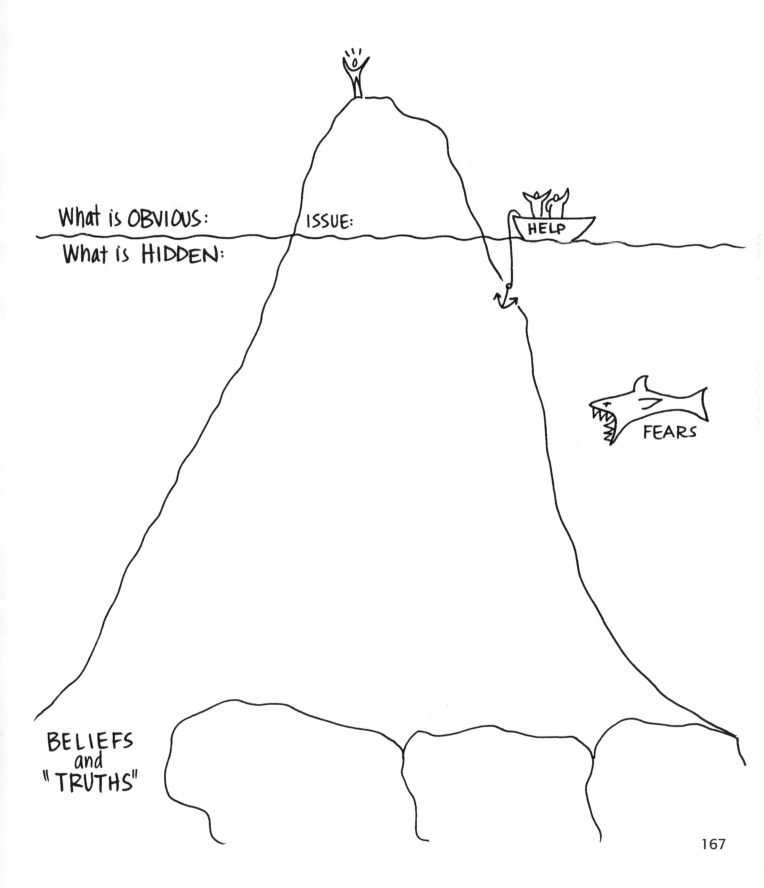

What is OBVIOUS:

ISSUE:

HELP

What is HIDDEN:

FEARS

BELIEFS
and
"TRUTHS"

Aspen Grove

Your students might be surprised to learn that one of the largest living organisms on Earth is an aspen grove. The trees that we see appear to be separate from each other, but what we don't see is the root system. Underground the trees are linked. Their roots form one giant system. Water and nutrients are shared along this system, keeping all the trees healthy.

Using the aspen grove as a metaphor, students can discover and record connections that are not apparent at first glance. If each tree were labeled with the name of one student, for example, what might show up in the root system that links all students? What root system connects a family, a community, a nation, or the entire planet?

You might also ask, "What keeps the root system alive? What can you do to ensure that the connections are healthy, growing, and strong?" Or, "What does the root system provide to make the individual trees healthy?"

The Aspen Grove template can be used in multiple ways in any classroom to explore the connections among seemingly separate entities: characters in a book, cultures, chemical elements, parts of an ecosystem, historical events, current events, the materials and tools required for building various objects, artistic movements, and so forth. Encourage students to fill out one before you begin teaching a subject, so that you can see at a glance what students already know. You will also learn what their preconceptions are, and your students will recognize just how much they already know (giving them confidence before starting the unit). Later they can compare what they have learned with what they knew before starting the unit, enhancing their sense of accomplishment. (See page 172 for the blank template.)

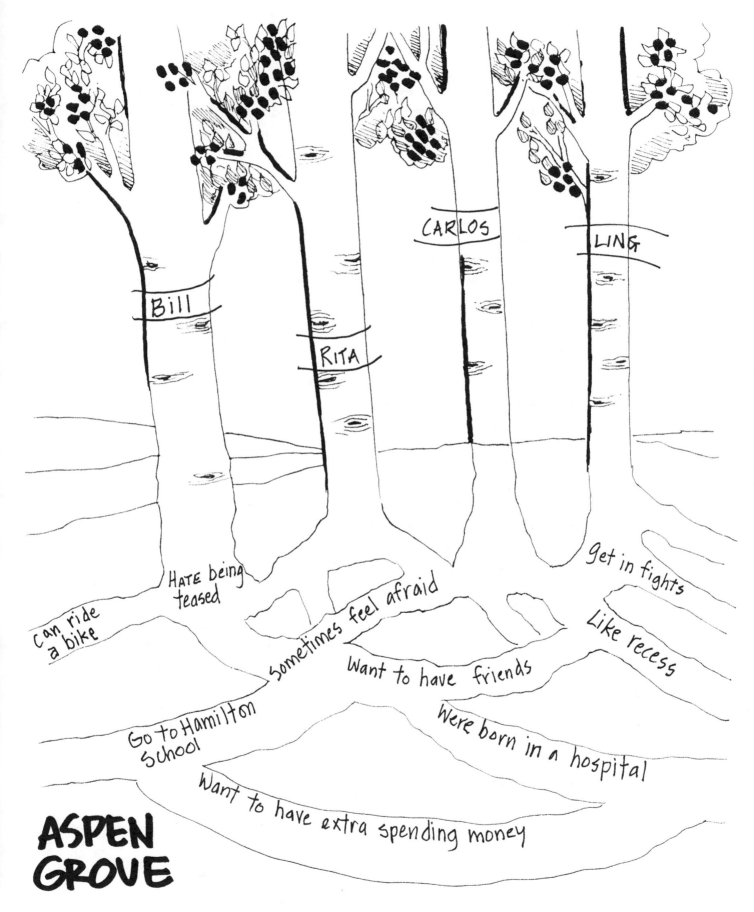

ASPEN GROVE

Aspen Grove Facts

When using the Aspen Grove template, you may wish to introduce your students to more facts about this amazing plant. Invite students to take notes by creating a Mindscape, as in the example on the opposite page. Notice that not every fact was selected for the Mindscape. Instead, each key element is represented. To map in greater detail, one could create a separate Mindscape for clonal roots or for aspen as nutrient.

- Aspens play an important role in the lives of an estimated 500 species, from bears to fungi. The leaves, twigs, and bark are highly nutritious, and deer and elk use them for overwintering since it's food they don't have to dig out of the snow. Black bears, cottontails, porcupines, and snowshoe hares feed on bark, buds, and foliage, and grouse and quail eat the winter buds.
- Small mammals, such as shrews, mice, and voles abound near aspens. Aspen is a favorite food and building material for the North American beaver.
- Aspen trees have what are called "clonal roots." Clonal roots are a group of genetically identical cells descended from a single common ancestor. The aspen's clonal roots send up suckers following a disturbance that clears space for sunlight. Fire is the chief agent, though avalanches, logging, and other disturbances are also part of the mix. These suckers become aspen trees, connected underground as part of one large organism.
- A mature root system can put out 400,000 to 1 million shoots per acre, and the sprouts can grow a meter per growing season initially. This easily outcompetes other tree species, which must regenerate from seed. Because aspens need full sun, the density of sprouts decreases as the canopy begins to shade out smaller seedlings.
- Individual aspen trees may live to 150 years in the western United States, and by this time, shade-tolerant conifers have grown taller than the aspen and begin to shade them out. Thus, aspen clones depend on periodic disturbance in order to maintain themselves.
- The age of such clones is not known, but it is commonly assumed that they go back to the last glaciation period, about 10,000 years ago.

Sources: Madson 1996 and Mitton and Grant 1996.

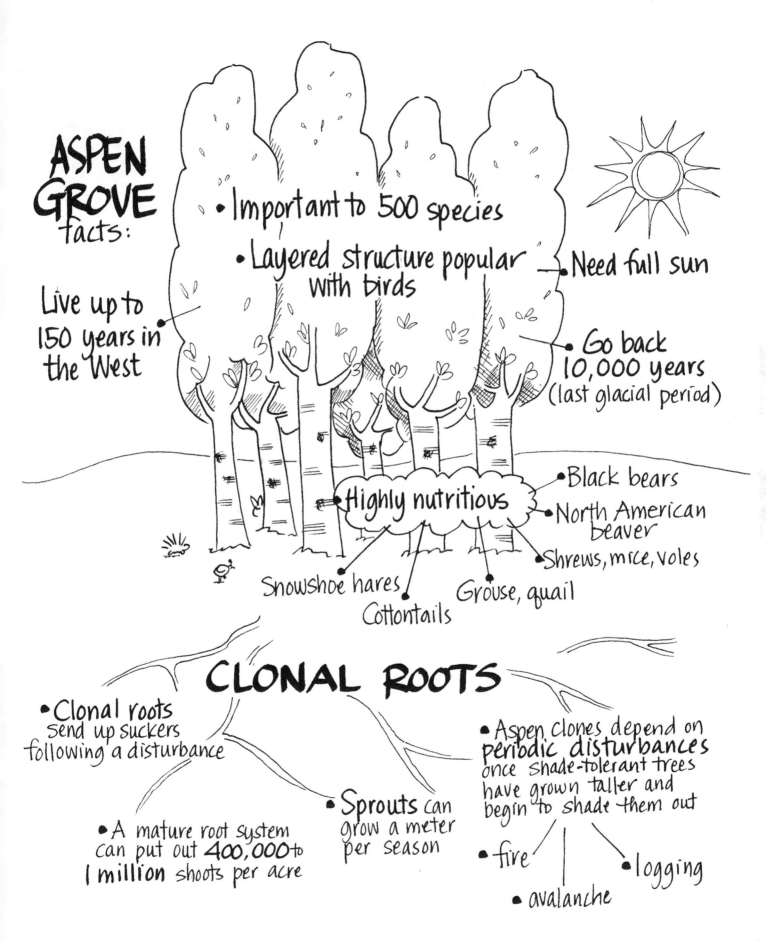

ASPEN GROVE facts:

- Important to 500 species
- Layered structure popular with birds

Need full sun

Live up to 150 years in the West

Go back 10,000 years (last glacial period)

Highly nutritious
- Black bears
- North American beaver
- Shrews, mice, voles

Snowshoe hares

Cottontails

Grouse, quail

CLONAL ROOTS

- Clonal roots send up suckers following a disturbance

- A mature root system can put out 400,000 to 1 million shoots per acre

- Sprouts can grow a meter per season

- Aspen clones depend on periodic disturbances once shade-tolerant trees have grown taller and begin to shade them out
  - fire
  - avalanche
  - logging

ASPEN
GROVE

Resources

Books

Adkins, Jan. 1978. *Symbols: A Silent Language.* New York: Walker and Company.

Brookes, Mona. 1996. *Drawing with Children: A Creative Method for Adult Beginners, Too.* New York: Jeremy P. Tarcher.

Caviglioli, Oliver, and Ian Harris. 2002. *Thinking Skills and Eye Q: Visual Clues for Raising Intelligence.* Model Learning Series. Stafford, UK: Network Educational Press.

———. 2003. *Thinking Visually.* Markham, ON: Pembroke Publishers.

Claxton, Guy. 2003. *Hare Brain, Tortoise Mind: How Intelligence Increases When You Think Less.* New York: Ecco Press.

Covey, Stephen R. 2004. *Seven Habits of Highly Effective People: Powerful Lessons in Personal Change.* New York: Frec Press.

De Bono, Edward. 1999. *Six Thinking Hats.* Revised and updated. Boston: Back Bay Books.

Emberley, Ed. 1975. *Ed Emberley's Drawing Book of Faces.* Boston: Little, Brown and Company.

Fontana, David. 1994. *The Secret Language of Symbols: A Visual Key to Symbols and Their Meanings.* San Francisco: Chronicle Books.

Gardner, Howard. 1999. *Intelligence Reframed: Multiple Intelligences for the 21st Century.* New York: Basic Books.

Gattegno, Caleb. 1969. *Towards a Visual Culture: Educating through Television.* New York: Outerbridge & Dienstfrey, distributed by Dutton.

Harris, Ian, and Oliver Caviglioli. 2003. *Think it—Map It! How Schools Use Mapping to Transform Teaching and Learning.* Model Learning Series. Stafford, UK: Network Educational Press.

Horn, Robert E. 1998. *Visual Language: Global Communication for the 21st Century.* Bainbridge Island, Wash.: MacroVU.

Hyerle, David. 1996. *Visual Tools for Constructing Knowledge.* Alexandria, Va.: Association for Supervision and Curriculum Development.

———. 2000. *A Field Guide to Using Visual Tools.* Alexandria, Va.: Association for Supervision and Curriculum Development.

Hyerle, David, ed. 2004. *Student Successes with Thinking Maps: School-Based Research, Results, and Models for Achievement Using Visual Tools.* Thousand Oaks, Calif.: Corwin Press.

Institute for the Advancement of Research in Education (IARE). 2003. *Graphic Organizers: A Review of Scientifically Based Research.* Report prepared for Inspiration Software. Charleston, W.Va.: AEL.

Levin, J. R. 1981. "On the Functions of Pictures in Prose." In *Neuropsychological and Cognitive Processes in Reading,* ed. Francis J. Pirozzolo and Merlin C. Wittrock. New York: Academic Press.

Lohr, Linda. 2003. *Creating Graphics for Learning and Performance: Lessons in Visual Literacy.* Upper Saddle River, N.J.: Merrill Prentice Hall.

Madson, Chris. 1996. "Trees Born of Fire and Ice." *National Wildlife* 34(6):28–35.

Margulies, Nancy. 1991. *Yes, You Can . . . Draw!* Tucson, Ariz.: Zephyr Press.

———. 1993. *Maps, Mindscapes and More.* VHS. Tucson, Ariz.: Zephyr Press.

———. 1995a. *Map It! Tools for Charting the Vast Territories of Your Mind.* Tucson, Ariz.: Zephyr Press.

———. 1995b. *Tools for Building Multiple Intelligences: The Magic 7.* Tucson, Ariz.: Zephyr Press.

Margulies, Nancy, with Nusa Maal. 2002. *Mapping Inner Space: Learning and Teaching Visual Mapping.* Tucson, Ariz.: Zephyr Press.

McGuinness, Carol. 2001. "Thinking Skills and Thinking Classrooms." Available online at http://www.scre.ac.uk/forum/forum2001/mcguiness.html. Accessed October 1, 2004.

Mitton, Jeffrey B., and Michael C. Grant. 1996. "Genetic Variation and the Natural History of Quaking Aspen." *BioScience* 46(1):25–31.

Moline, Steve. 1995. *I See What You Mean: Children at Work with Visual Information.* York, Maine: Stenhouse Publishers.

Sibbet, David. 1991. *Fundamentals of Graphic Language.* Graphic Guides. San Francisco: Grove Consultants International.

———. 1994. *Pocket Pics.* San Francisco: Grove Consultants International.

Valenza, Christine. 1994. *Meeting Magic: Presentation Graphics for Results, a Reference Book.* Lafayette, Calif.: Bright Ideas Press.

Wurman, Richard S. 1990. *Information Anxiety.* London: Pan.

Organizations and People

Susan Kelly is a graphic facilitator and visual practitioner in the San Francisco Bay area. Contact her at 415-550-8781.

Michelle Boos-Stone is a corporate Mindscape artist.

> Gecko Graphics
> 8100 East Topia Street
> Long Beach, CA 90808
> 562-598-7840
> mboos13@aol.com

Greg Gollaher is the creator of Greg's people (on page 38)

> 916-691-3973
> www.gollaherconsulting.com

Since 1980, **New Horizons for Learning** has served as a leading-edge resource for educational change: http://newhorizons.org/. Dee Dickinson, who wrote the foreword to this book, established New Horizons. Her website receives more than 5 million hits per week.

After ten years of work with diverse groups and individuals, **Nusa Maal** founded SenseSmart in order to provide experiences, processes, and products to engage a broader bandwidth of natural human intelligence.

> SenseSmart Consulting International
> 8317 North Brook Lane, Suite 1007
> Bethesda, MD 20814
> info@sensesmart.com
> www.SenseSmart.com

Visualpractitioner.org is a website forum for visual practitioners from all over the globe: http://www.visualpractitioner.org/

Reinhard Kuchenmueller and Dr. Marianne Stifel of **Visuelle Protokolle,** in Germany, help you to find the right pictures for your topics and use pictures to facilitate and coach, helping people find their inner pictures: www.visuelle-protokolle.de.

175

Index